"IT WAS A TOUGH YEAR . . .

"But, here's the thing—I now look back on that year with a great deal of fondness! Weird, but true. And not an uncommon sentiment. . . . Most of the women I know who have had breast cancer came to regard it as a challenge. We adapted, coped, and learned to fit cancer into our schedules so that it became something we could handle physically, mentally, and practically. In the process, we discovered new and wonderful things about ourselves and others. . . . It was an Outward Bound for the soul.

"Happiness and well-being are not guaranteed side effects of breast-cancer treatment. They are things you have to work at, just as you will work on minimizing the more unpleasant side effects of chemo and radiation. This book will help you do both. It is a practical guide that will take you step by step through those scary-sounding treatments—the chemo and radiation that often come after surgery for breast cancer. This book is designed to help you avoid or cope with the unpleasant stuff, and also to lift your spirits and help you find strength and wisdom through your experience."

—*from BREAST CANCER,*
THERE AND BACK

BREAST CANCER

THERE AND BACK

A WOMAN~TO~WOMAN GUIDE

JAMI BERNARD

FOREWORD BY **CLIFFORD HUDIS • M.D.,** CHIEF, BREAST CANCER
MEDICINE SERVICE, MEMORIAL SLOAN-KETTERING CANCER CENTER

WARNER BOOKS

An AOL Time Warner Company

Copyright © 2001 by Jami Bernard
All rights reserved.

Warner Books, Inc., 1271 Avenue of the Americas, New York, NY 10020
Visit our Web site at www.twbookmark.com.
For information on Time Warner Trade Publishing's online publishing program, visit www.ipublish.com.

 An AOL Time Warner Company

Printed in the United States of America

First Printing: October 2001

10 9 8 7 6 5 4 3 2 1

Library of Congress Cataloging-in-Publication Data
Bernard, Jami.
    Breast cancer, there and back : a woman-to-woman guide / Jami Bernard.
       p. cm.
    Includes bibliographical references.
    ISBN 0-446-67753-1
    1. Breast—Cancer—Popular works. I Title.

RC280.B8 B45 2001
616.99'449—dc21   2001017943

Cover design by Mary Ann Smith
Book design by Charles Sutherland

This book is dedicated with gratitude to the medical team
who saved my life:

Dr. Clifford Hudis, medical oncologist
Dr. Jeanne Petrek, surgeon
Dr. Beryl McCormack, radiation oncologist

Acknowledgments

Have laptop, will travel. Portions of this book were written at a succession of my friends' weekend homes. Thank you, Bruce Cohen (Water Mill), for the hammock, tech support, gourmet meals, and Billie Holliday piped into my bedroom. Thank you, Donna Dickman and Merrick Bursuk (Greenport) for the peach pie and the blizzard adventure. Thank you, Marianne Goldstein and Donald Berman (Pine Plains) for the frosty cocktails on the lawn. Thank you, Diane Stefani and Terry Peikin (Berkshires) for the various "working weekends" in which most of the work involved strapping the kayak to the top of the car. Thank you, Dorrie Crockett, for Thanksgiving in Vegas and all the study-hall sessions interrupted only by creativity-enhancing snacks.

Amanda and Peter Low, I know the guest cottage renovations weren't finished in time for this book. You did what you could. But don't worry. Next book.

While I was toiling away in country-house bliss, Marie Menendez was whistling to my parrot, Sensei, and later kept me on track by teaching me the zen of opening a pomegranate. JoAnne Wasserman took my hand and never let me walk alone in Cancer World, even when it hurt her to do so. The steadfastly supportive

Dave Kehr took the terror out of going back to work when I wasn't sure I was up to it. A big group hug goes to the women from my support group, all of whom continue to be friends along this bumpy ride.

And there are more: My agent, Elaine Markson, makes everything possible. The thoughtful contributions and steady hand of my editor, Karen Melnyk, made this book a true collaboration. Gwen Darien and the staff of *Mamm* magazine gave me an opportunity to test-drive some of my wilder ideas about breast-cancer humor. And Baram (Ramy) Kim, my medical research assistant, is the bright light of the future—smart, funny, beautiful, sweet, and still so young!

Other people who watched my back during the writing of this book were my colleague Jack Mathews, who is a pleasure to work with (and who also has the good sense to have a parrot); my sister, Diane Bernard; and my mother, Gloria Bernard. Lance Gould helped block those metaphors, and he has the bruises to prove it.

I now have dual citizenship here and in Cancer World, and I thank the many people I've met in both places who have eased my travels.

Contents

Author's Note

This book is not intended to be a substitute for medical care and advice. You are advised to consult with your health care professional about matters relating to your health, including particular matters relating to the diagnosis and treatment of breast cancer.

The information provided in this book is based upon sources that the author believes to be reliable. All such information regarding specific products and companies is current as of January 2001.

FOREWORD

By CLIFFORD HUDIS, M.D.

Chief, Breast Cancer Medicine Service,
Memorial Sloan-Kettering Cancer Center

A diagnosis of breast cancer is always scary. Some handle the news with aplomb. Others break down and hear nothing else for weeks or longer. Some interpret the diagnosis as a mountain to conquer, a busy street to cross, or a distraction from the real business of life.

Regardless, the flood of information available to the public and the heightened awareness of women's health issues in the past few decades has not necessarily made such a diagnosis any easier or less scary. All of us, plumbers and painters, teachers and even doctors, can experience the same overwhelming emotions and turmoil on first hearing that we, or someone we love, has cancer, and our first instinct may be to try and take control.

Yet this is inherently an uncontrollable situation. There's the basic deranged biology of the cancer cell, there are busy doctors and impersonal health care delivery systems, and there's the rest of your life to manage. All these things appear to be at odds with each other. This seeming loss of control and fear of future uncertainties can be overwhelming, no matter how educated and prepared you think you are.

Where do you turn? To the well-meaning friend? The comforting relative? The dispassionate doctor? Your friend's spouse, the internist? Added to this is the press of time. You *have* to do something about this cancer diagnosis tonight! Or so it seems. How do you gather the resources needed to begin and complete this journey in a timely but accurate manner?

These questions lead many people to different answers, but it always boils down to a quest for the right kind of information at the right time, delivered in a useful form. There is no one way to best accomplish this. For some, it's an exhaustive search of the National Library of Medicine and discussions with experts and mavens around the world. For others it's a conversation with a trusted and skilled physician, and that's all it takes. For many people, their information needs to change and grow over the days and weeks after they first learn that they may have breast cancer. Worries about finding time to schedule surgery are replaced by worries about survival and then by worries about appearance or sexuality or exercise tolerance. No matter how things unfold, there are always worries to deal with and plans to make along the way.

The question is, how does each individual approach these problems and get the needed information? In fact, it is this step that does the most to restore control. The best possible treatment allows you the best chance to control the cancer. The best possible support, be it medical or social or psychiatric, allows you to take back some control of your life.

There are numerous resources now available for a woman diagnosed with cancer, and the world is better for it. You can join a chat room on the Web or visit numerous Web sites. You can call an 800 number and talk to a volunteer, or you can talk to one or many doctors and nurses and other health care professionals. You can read a textbook or a guidebook. But in the quiet of the evening, when you just want to sit, think, and absorb at your own pace, where can you turn?

At diagnosis, my patient Jami Bernard was hungry for information, like many readers of this book. But she needed it delivered a certain way. It had to be accurate—she seems to have no patience for nonsense—it had to be helpful, and it had to be approachable. *Breast Cancer, There and Back* is Jami's response to her journey into what she has called "Cancer World," and it will be a great resource and comfort to women and their families facing the same trip. It is friendly, funny, and fact-filled, without being too dense.

This book tells you why you feel what you may feel during treatment, what may help, and what may not. It offers sensible questions to ask and alternatives to consider. The reasons for the different treatments and ways to cope with their side effects are explained in a simple yet accurate fashion in these pages. The air of good humor, sensible advice, and accurate medical data, present throughout the book, should provide comfort and reassurance for those of you facing this challenge.

I wish you a quick and painless journey through "Cancer World," if you're forced to go. And I hope that if you do have to go, you emerge as Jami did, wiser and stronger for having been there.

PREFACE

As I write this, I am approaching the fifth anniversary of my breast cancer diagnosis. According to the statistics to which I decided to cling during my initial panic, there was a good chance I would not have gotten this far without a recurrence. And yet, here I am, cancer free and feeling fine!

Mine is not an isolated case. Science and medicine are getting more of a handle on cancer every day. Meanwhile, there are highly effective treatments for breast cancer. As cumbersome and unpleasant as they can seem, they are actually miracles of modern medicine, because they enable you to reach a day that seemed unthinkable—the day when the stark details of what you went through begin to fade from memory.

If you are reading this, then doubtless you (or someone you love) are embarking on a journey I know only too well. My guess is that you have so many thoughts and feelings jostling for position that your head is spinning. You're frightened. Anxious. Perhaps you're resigned to what's ahead of you, perhaps you're curious, at times you're angry. You feel confident one moment ("I can handle this!") and a teary wreck the next ("Why me?"). You're confused. You'd like to make it all go away but the noise in your head won't even let you escape through sleep. Your friends and family are being wonderful and annoying at the same time. When they ask a simple "How *are* you?," you may lash out in a rage and not know why. You wonder if life will ever go back to normal.

In fact, you can't remember what "normal" is, because from the moment of your diagnosis until the end of your treatments, you're living in Cancer World. I know, because I've been there . . . and back.

I'm a film critic for the *New York Daily News*. My only experience with breast cancer was through the fiction of movies. There were hardly any at the time that even touched on the topic, with the exception of the occasional circumspect reference.

In February 1996 I went to my doctor to check out a lump I'd noticed while swimming in the Bahamas. The lump was on the side of my left breast and it was red, swollen, and extremely painful. I had decided it must be a sunburn, and with this level of denial in place I was able to enjoy the rest of my vacation. My friends said it was probably nothing, because breast cancer is usually diffi-cult to detect and painless. But this lump that seemed to have come out of nowhere (that's how I described it at the time and the phrase was written on my chart—I peeked) turned out upon inspection to be malignant. I had a fine-needle biopsy one morning and by 4 P.M., when the surgeon called right on schedule to report the alarming news, my life changed.

How did I feel? It was like answering the door in your bathrobe with unwashed hair and realizing you'd invited twenty guests over for a formal dinner. I was flustered, unprepared, agitated. Of all the things I thought might happen to me, breast cancer had never entered my mind, especially since I wasn't yet forty and had always thought of breast cancer as a diagnosis for the elderly. I knew nothing about the disease, the treatments, or what I was in for.

That year I received a record number of flowers on Valentine's Day, the day after my lumpectomy. That's the way life goes—one day, you're making Top Ten movie lists and swimming in the Bahamas, two weeks later you're packing your fuzzy koala slippers for a trip to the hospital. The surgery was followed by nine months of chemo and seven weeks of radiation. I spent an entire year in what I called Cancer World, a year in which my daily schedule and thoughts all swirled around the subject of cancer. Every day was filled with some cancer-related activity, or so it seemed. If I wasn't on my way to a treatment, I was recovering from one, or managing a side effect, or getting up to speed on this new subject that seemed to have overtaken my life. I lived in Cancer World for all of 1996, and it was a tough year.

But, here's the thing—I now look back on that year with a great deal of fondness! Weird, but true. And not an uncommon sentiment. In the same way that I regard the telltale seam on my breast as a reminder of how great it is to be alive, I think back on Cancer World and remember how generous my friends and family were, how interesting and vivid that year was, how well I rose to the occasion, how focused I was on recovery and being kind to myself, and what an interesting challenge it all was. Most of the women I know who have had breast cancer came to regard it thus. We adapted, coped, and learned to fit cancer into our schedules so that it became something we could handle physically, mentally, and practically. In the process, we discovered new and wonderful things about ourselves and others. It enabled us to cement relationships, helped us set priorities and redefine goals, and made us extraordinarily aware of how precious life is. It was an Outward Bound for the soul.

The cancer itself was only a small part of Cancer World. The rest of it was about living through unusual circumstances. To continue the analogy of the sudden dinner party, this book won't cook the food for you, but it's full of recipes for how to get through the evening.

There's always something magical about the five-year anniversary after any cancer diagnosis, and I'm enjoying the sound of it, even though all of us in the "sisterhood" know how precarious a thing health is. No mortal is immune to the occasional breakdown of the body or its defenses. But if you learn to regard cancer treatment not as a punishment but as a process—and a temporary one at that—then you can learn to incorporate it into your life. Would you choose this for yourself? No. Can you handle it? Yes!

Of all the curveballs life can throw (and curveballs are such a staple of life that you'd best keep practicing your swing), breast cancer turned out to be something I managed with far more dignity and grace than I had brought to such prior catastrophes as hangnails and breakups. I learned a lot about myself from going through the treatments. I learned about what I want from life and how I prefer to spend my time. I enjoy life more and make time for the little things that give me pleasure, like reading in bed, learning new sports, and taking ridiculously luxurious baths.

Don't get me wrong—happiness and well-being are not guaranteed side effects of breast-cancer treatment. They are things you have to work at, if you choose to, just as you will work on minimizing the more unpleasant side effects of chemo and radiation. This book will help you do both. It is a practical guide that will take you step by step through those two scary-sounding treatments— the chemo and radiation that often come after surgery for breast cancer. This book is designed to help you avoid or cope with the unpleasant stuff, and also to lift your spirits and help you find strength and wisdom through your experience.

—Jami Bernard, New York City, 2000

PART ONE

THE BASICS

1

❁

Introduction to Chemotherapy
and Radiation

Chemotherapy* and/or **radiation therapy** are two types of treatment commonly given to **breast-cancer** patients in addition to surgery. The surgery physically removes the **tumor**, while the chemo and radiation kill off stray **cancer cells** that may still be lurking in the area or have traveled through the **lymphatic system** to other parts of the body. If you have picked up this book, then not only are you preparing for chemo and/or radiation treatments, but you are also exhibiting extraordinary literary taste, and for that I congratulate you.

Getting chemo isn't a walk in the park, but on the scale of things that make me nauseous, it still beats a tax audit. There are fabulous new designer drugs available to help you get through chemo (some patients don't ever throw up!), whereas if you are audited, very few drugs will alleviate your pain.

---

*Glossary words are marked in boldface upon first reference.

Science is making breakthroughs every day in treating cancer, breast cancer in particular. When caught in the early stages, it is so treatable it's considered curable. Meanwhile, chemo and radiation (in addition to surgery and synthetic **hormones** such as **tamoxifen**) are the best weapons in the modern world's breast cancer arsenal.

Yet it all sounds so frightening. Radiation seems scary because if you didn't pay attention back in science class, then you haven't the foggiest idea of how and why it works. Chemo, on the other hand, is not such a mystery. Everyone has an opinion on chemo, and it's usually not a good one. The prospect of going through chemo can be more troublesome to many people than the cancer itself. When the surgeon who performed my **lumpectomy** told me that I'd need chemo, I blanched and said this was the first *I'd* heard of it, when in fact we had discussed it a mere two days before. I had blocked the memory of that discussion entirely and was in such denial that I thought my surgeon was pulling a fast one.

A BRIEF HISTORY OF BREAST CANCER—OR, BE THANKFUL YOU WEREN'T BORN WAY BACK WHEN

Boy, are you lucky, all things considered. It wasn't until the sixteenth century that anatomy became a science, so surgery before that time was largely based on folk wisdom. Be grateful you were not born before the mid-nineteenth century, when **anesthetics** and antiseptics were first discovered. Until then, a patient was lucky to get a shot of whiskey before being cut open.

If you think chemo sounds bad, at least it's proven to be effective, unlike the treatments of yore. It would not be wise to get breast cancer in France in 1350, where you might be prescribed "an infusion of elderberry roots pickled in vinegar for nine days." Marilyn Yalom, in her book *A History of the Breast*, lists just a few of the horrible mixtures smeared on breasts in the name of medicine in ages past, including burned excrement of men, wasps, or bats; cow's brain; crawfish boiled in ass's milk; pork blood, arsenic, lead, and mercury ointments; compresses dipped in urine; rotten apples; and vivisected pigeon parts.

The first surgeon to add **axillary dissection** to breast surgery (removal of **lymph nodes** under the arm), even before the lymphatic system was discovered, was the German surgeon Wilhelm Fabry at the turn of the seventeenth century, when it was still thought that breast cancer was caused by breast milk that had curdled and hardened. "For the next 200 years, medicine and quackery, superstition and science, unfounded prejudice and empirical observation coexisted willy-nilly, as they still do, if less flagrantly, in our own time," writes Yalom. Her descriptions of old-time folk remedies are reminiscent of some of today's superstitions, such as trying to cure cancer with herbal tea or positive thinking.

Chemo, by comparison, has the clear advantage of being effective in a predictable percentage of cases, a percentage clearly higher than would be the case if you did nothing. It was initially used as an **adjuvant treatment** in the 1960s. You can see why chemo got such a bad rap. Before better **antiemetic** drugs were discovered to prevent nausea, many patients spent the better part of their time camped out in their bathrooms. The fear of treatment—of the time it takes, the hassle, the laundry list of possible side effects—can feel more devastating than the treatment itself.

I'm a firm believer in the adage knowledge is power. The more you know about why and how these treatments work and what to expect, the better you will be able to cope with them and be a proactive patient who participates in her own recovery. (Only 1 percent of breast-cancer patients are men, so guys, if you're reading this, you'll just have to put up with the feminine pronoun throughout this book.)

I'm not recommending that you go overboard and get a doctoral degree in **oncology.** I'm just saying that a lot of the fear of cancer treatments has to do with fear of the unknown.

So let's demystify the process!

✳ WEIRD FACT

The most famous midwife in Paris during the early 1600s was Madame Louise Bourgeois, who brought Louis XIII into the world. Here is Madame's Rx for breast cancer, according to *A History of the Breast*: "Take a half-pound of lard and dissolve it, a small amount of new wax, two ounces of pitch [tar], and from all of this make an ointment, with which you will plaster the breast once it has been lanced."

CHEMO 101

For many breast cancer patients, chemo is the next step after surgery. Chemo and radiation are both very intensive and their cumulative impact makes you tired, so doctors typically administer them separately. One advantage of leaving radiation for last is that it gives your breast more time to heal after surgery, but the order in which you receive the two may be a function of the policy of your hospital, or whether your cancer is **estrogen-receptor** positive. In some cases, chemo is given even before surgery to reduce the size of the tumor.

Chemo is a "systemic" treatment (because it travels throughout your system) that is administered either in pill form or through an IV (intravenous needle). There are different kinds of chemo and different chemo combinations, or "cocktails." What they basically do is kill off fast-growing cells by interfering with the rogue cells' ability to divide. Cancer cells are fast-growing cells; unlike my own mathematical abilities, they divide and multiply with lightning speed. Eventually, they crowd out the normal cells, preventing the body from performing its necessary functions.

Chemo singles out fast-growing cells and says to them, "Can't you read the sign? This is a no-dividing, no-multiplying zone! Move along!"

However, the chemo cannot differentiate between the "bad" fast-growing cells and the "good" fast-growing cells, which happen to be the ones in the digestive tract, the reproductive organs, the **bone marrow** (where new blood cells are manufactured), and the hair follicles. This explains some of chemo's famous side effects, like runny nose, upset stomach, low blood counts, and hair loss. The amount or type of side effects you get are not an indication of how and whether the chemo is working, but of how your body happens to respond under the circumstances.

Chemo is administered (generally on an out-patient basis) in "cycles," meaning that the body gets to recover a bit (usually three or four weeks) before the next infusion. Shorter cycles are now possible using new bone marrow stimulants, but these are not considered standard at present. Four doses, then, would typically take about three months.

Like all cells, cancer cells go through growth phases. The exact effect of various chemotherapy agents is not always the same and the mechanisms by which they kill cells is not necessarily known. In general, scientists think chemo attacks cancer cells before they are able to divide. Since different cells are at different growth phases at different times, the chemo kills off cancer cells in waves, then hits others during the next round of treatments, etc. The first blast of chemo wipes out as many cancer cells as possible. After that, the chemo continues to "stalk malignant cells," as one book describes the process, which brings to mind chemo molecules in hunting caps and red-plaid jackets. In fact, scientists believe that the same proportion of cells are killed with each dose. However, this presents a problem similar to the man who halves the distance home with each step—he never actually gets there!

In addition, cells may grow back after each treatment.

The hope is that enough cycles of effective treatment will kill enough cancer cells to allow other bodily defenses to limit growth of cancer cells.

In addition to being "systemic," chemo is also called an "adjuvant" treatment for breast cancer because it is administered in addition to surgery. (Radiation, however, is considered a "primary" treatment, and is almost always given to women who have had lumpectomies, and occasionally to women who have had mastectomies.)

The key motivation for the use of chemotherapy (and hormone therapy, too) is that, unlike surgery and radiation treatments which are aimed at identified sites of cancer, chemo is unaimed and can attack cancer wherever it might be lurking in the body.

Years ago, it was assumed that if few or no lymph nodes were involved (diagnosed "positive"), then the cancer hadn't spread to any other parts of the body. The lymph nodes were considered the tollbooths on the cancer highway, and if they hadn't seen any traffic yet, it was assumed you were relatively safe.

Later it was found that cancer cells could break away at any time and wander past your internal "no trespassing" signs, even when a tumor was in its early stages. These stray cancer cells, while invisible to imaging methods like X rays, could set up shop elsewhere, most notably in the liver or bones, thus **metastasizing** (or spreading) the original cancer to other parts of the body. When this happens, the far-flung cancer is still known as "breast cancer," no matter where in the body it shows up.

Because of these discoveries, today's breast cancer patients very often get chemo if only as an insurance policy, just in case a cell or two escaped and is on the lam.

CHEMO COCKTAILS: RECIPE FOR HEALTH

There are dozens of chemotherapy drugs available to fight cancer. Here is a list of the most common chemo "cocktails," or combinations, given to breast cancer patients. Granted, they are not as appealing as such cocktails as the chocolate martini.

CMF: Cyclophosphamide (marketed as Cytoxan), methotrexate, 5-fluorouracil (5-FU)

CAF: Cyclophosphamide, doxorubicin (Adriamycin), 5-fluorouracil

CEF: Cyclophosphamide, epirubicin, 5-fluorouracil

CMFVP: Cyclophosphamide, methotrexate, 5-fluorouracil, vincristine, prednisone

AC: Doxorubicin, cyclophosphamide

VAT: Vinblastine, doxorubicin, thiotepa

VATH: Vinblastine, doxorubicin, thiotepa, fluoxymesterone

CDDP + VP-16: Cisplatin, etoposide, mitomycin C plus vinblastine

AC + T: Doxorubicin and cyclophosphamide followed by paclitaxel

AC + Txt: Doxorubicin and cyclophosphamide followed by docetaxel

Chemo is often administered in cocktails because it has been found that these combinations are far more effective than using any of the agents singly. However, even that conclusion is currently under very careful study. As noted in the doctors' reference book *Principles of Cancer Management: Chemotherapy*, "Although such selection leads to a wider range of side effects, it minimizes the risk of a lethal effect caused by multiple insults to the same organ system by different drugs and allows dose intensity to be maximized."

My own chemo regimen involved three months of Adriamycin and six months of CMF, the latter of which I dubbed "chemo lite" because it allowed my hair to grow back.

"Adria" was the chemo I liked least. The name sounded so pretty and it came in a cheerful orange color, but it is quite potent and needs to be administered with plenty of IV fluids so that it doesn't sclerose (scar) the vein. It's also part of the chemo family that, at typical doses, is guaranteed to make you lose your hair—other types may just thin it.

Your doctor will custom tailor your chemo regimen based on a number of factors. Some of these factors have to do with your original tumor, such as how large it was or whether any lymph nodes under the arm were involved. The type and amount of chemo you get is also dependent on your age and general health. The oncologist will factor in risk versus reward when designing the length and aggressiveness of your treatment. If you've lived a long, full life, you may not want to spend a precious six months undergoing chemo.

How much chemo you can tolerate is initially formulated according to the measurement of your body surface and later refined as treatments progress. Your doctor will know how well it's working not by how many side effects you get, but by the measurable evidence in your blood counts.

QUESTIONS TO ASK YOUR ONCOLOGIST

- How many patients have you treated with similar cases?
- Why do I need this treatment?
- How long will this treatment take?
- What is my prognosis? (This is a tricky question, because the oncologist needs to be frank without unduly alarming you. Still, you have a right to know what he thinks about your particular case, and how other women fared with similar treatments. Just keep in mind that an answer to this question is only an estimate based on comparison with huge swaths of the population.)
- What are my options regarding chemo, and do I have other options besides chemo?
- Why are you recommending this particular chemo regimen? (Most chemo regimens are standard, the difference being in the amount an individual receives. But the doctor may have a philosophy about treatment that you'll be interested to hear.)
- What are the possible side effects, and when do they show up?
- Who do I call to help me manage the side effects? The oncologist? A nurse? A resident on duty at the hospi-

tal if it's after 5 P.M.? If so, is there a separate phone number?

- What are the side effects that are considered serious enough for hospitalization?
- Are there any longer-term side effects I need to be aware of?
- When can I go back to work or resume normal activities?
- Will I also be given hormonal treatments, like tamoxifen, and if so, what additional side effects can I expect?
- Will I cease to menstruate during chemo? If so, will it begin again? When?
- Will the sum total of these treatments affect my ability to conceive?
- Are there other issues regarding future pregnancy I need to be aware of?

RADIATION 101

Radiation is similar to chemo in that it interrupts fast-growing cells and prevents them from getting what they need in order to keep dividing. With **external-beam radiation**, a stream of high-energy particles or waves is aimed at the affected breast in order to kill off any stray cancer cells that might have escaped the surgeon's scalpel.

Radiation also has its own list of side effects, including a temporary sunburn that makes you look like you wore only half your bikini top at the beach. But you absolutely cannot feel radiation being administered. There is no pain or discomfort. Since it's aimed at the breast and nowhere else, it does not cause the digestive problems commonly associated with radiation for other kinds of cancer.

And, needless to say, you will not glow in the dark or develop X-ray vision. The reality of radiation is not nearly as exciting as your fertile imagination may suggest.

External-beam radiation is like getting an X ray. A machine aims the beams at your breast while you lie on a table. On rare occasions, a doctor may recommend **brachytherapy,** or **internal radiation,** in which little pellets of iridium 192 are implanted through plastic tubes right in the breast tissue itself. Picture those TV commercials for time-release allergy medication, and you get the idea. If you do receive brachytherapy, it will be in a hospital setting, and—don't take it personally, it's not your breath—your guests will have to sit six feet away to avoid exposure to that small amount of radiation.

QUESTIONS FOR YOUR RADIATION ONCOLOGIST

- How does radiation work?
- Why do I need radiation?
- How much radiation will I receive?
- How long will the treatments take?
- Will I receive a radiation "boost" at the end of treatment?
- What are the possible side effects?
- Are there any long-term risks associated with this treatment?
- Are there any vitamins or supplements I should specif-

ically avoid during treatment? Are there any I should take?
- Who do I call to help me manage the side effects? What if it's after business hours?
- Will I be able to go to work?
- Will these treatments affect my ability to conceive in the future?

CONCLUSION

Chemo and radiation treatments are time-intensive, but that's a good thing. Believe me, you do *not* want all those treatments in one sitting.

The treatments are tough on the body, and the body needs time to recuperate between doses. So chemo is usually given in several sittings spaced three weeks or so apart—the interval should be consistent for maximum effect—and radiation is given for a few minutes once a day for about six weeks. Everyone's treatment is different, but I know that mine took just about a year door-to-door, from diagnosis and surgery to the day I hopped off the radiation table and yelled, "So long, suckers!" (Well, I *thought* about yelling it.)

I could be melodramatic and say it was a year out of my life, but it was not. It was a year *added* to my life. I went back to work full time after my first chemo treatment and finished writing a book. I socialized, dated, and did just about all the things I usually do. Although my life was taken up with breast cancer, it was a full and rewarding year nonetheless. A difficult year? Yes, but as I often reminded myself, it was *only* difficult, not *impossible*.

✳ FINDING A GOOD "FIT" WITH YOUR DOCTOR

My mother was raised during an era when all doctors were considered gods. You dressed nicely for a visit with them, you didn't pester them, and you kept all those nagging questions to yourself. My mother thinks they're all geniuses, even if they went to off-shore med schools. It's touching, really.

I have a different view of doctors. They were the kids I went to school with who chose a different career track, one that was open to anyone with the inclination and grades. These kids were as silly and immature and flawed as any of us, but they chose a career that carried a great deal of responsibility. That probably sobered them up fast.

No matter the field of endeavor, medicine included, there will be a bell curve of the few who excel to greatness, the competent majority, and the strugglers who bring up the rear. I know that if your waiter isn't up to snuff, you won't think twice about trying a different restaurant next time. As a consumer, you have the same right to choose your doctor.

It's not that I don't respect doctors. I also respect a good cabdriver who knows the route and gets me there safely. People who love their work, take it seriously, and pay attention to the nuances are tops in any profession. You can't walk into a doctor's office so cowed by the medical degree on the wall that you forget to ask questions or to demand respect in return.

You'll have a long relationship with your oncologist, because there will be follow-up visits every three months, then every six months, and finally on an annual basis. So it has got to be someone who is not only professional, but also someone with whom you are comfortable.

Getting a second opinion is your right as a patient, and you may want to get one if only to find a doctor you like better personally. One friend of mine even got a third opinion; her first doctor frightened her, the second one seemed distracted, but the third time was a charm. I never went for a second opinion, but that was a conscious choice I made because I was comfortable with the doctor, his staff, the facilities, and the course of treatment. I was already happy with my surgeon, and the two were part of the same medical group.

On the other hand, this is your oncologist, not your new best friend. Liking your doctor does not mean you have to agree on politics, literature, or fashion.

GOOD DOCTORS . . .

- Are professional without being cold and severe.
- Are knowledgeable and patient.
- Answer all your questions.
- Look you in the eye.
- Make the time for you without constantly checking their watches.
- Treat their nurses and staff with respect.
- Give you a good feeling.
- Don't let you cool your heels in the waiting room too long.

2

Chemo, Day One

If you're one of those people who don't want to be a bother to others, cut it out right now! Your friends, family, and neighbors are there to help, and this is one time you could really use the company.

From a practical standpoint, you may need someone to take you home afterward in case you are depleted or groggy—the sedatives they may give you in your IV could make you too loopy to file a nail, let alone operate a clutch. Think of this person as your chemo companion. From a nonpractical standpoint, it is simply comforting to have someone with you, or near you. Think of how it is when you have the flu. You'd like someone near enough to make you a cup of tea but not so near that they hover and make you nervous. Above all, there are times in life when you just want someone to take you home and tuck you in, and these small kindnesses go far toward taking the sting out of what you're going through.

In most cases, the chemo process itself takes only about forty-five minutes (although some regimens may take a few hours), with most of that time taken up by such housekeeping details as finding a vein, running IV fluids, etc. If it were only 45 minutes out of your day, it might not be so bad. But this isn't a McDonald's drive-thru. Most of your day will be spent sitting around waiting for the oncologist to see you or the nurse to draw your blood or the receptionist to complete your paperwork and give you another appointment. On treatment days, block out a huge amount of time rather than feel rushed to make it to your next appointment.

Ideally, your chemo companion should be someone who is supportive yet doesn't drive you crazy. Sometimes this rules out family members, who can get even more upset than you are and whose anxiety can run through your veins like an IV drip. My chemo companions were usually my mother, my sister, or my friend JoAnne Wasserman, each of whom had a different waiting-room personality. My sister, Diane, kept up a running commentary, notable for its high degree of giddiness. Sometimes I tuned in and laughed along. Other times I tuned out and barely heard a word she said—she didn't seem to notice. She was like my own personal white-noise machine, blocking out any unpleasant feelings I was having. JoAnne treated me the way she treated her then six-year-old son—she patted my arm, wiggled my knee, and occasionally engaged me in distracting conversation. She now claims I was very witty in the waiting room, and even recites some of my one-liners, but I have no recollection of this. My brilliant chemo-era thoughts are now irretrievable.

My mom . . . well, my mom drove me crazy. That's her job. She worried about me and I worried about her worrying about me. I know she desperately wanted to be there for me, but my illness was tough on her in ways too complicated to deal with at the time.

If your family is out of town and your friends are at work, don't be embarrassed to turn to neighbors. Undoubtedly a few of them have already offered to help, and, you know what? They mean it! Helping neighbors in times of trouble is one of the most rewarding things people can do for each other, and such things often lead to new friendships and an important sense of community. You'll be amazed at how often even virtual strangers will want to be of assistance. Since my recovery, I have gone along with friends to their consultations and their treatments, and although they were surprised and grateful, they never suspected that I do this for myself! I enjoy giving back whatever I can, because so many people were so good to me in my own time of need. I'm not a sentimental person, but I get pretty teary over this.

Some hospitals and cancer centers have outreach programs that can provide you with a buddy for your visits. You have only to ask.

It bears repeating that what works for one person may not work for another. Bring someone with whom you are comfortable enough so that you don't have to put on your best face. But don't feel bad that this is not always the person you love best or spend the most time with.

Sometimes patients bond with each other during chemo and fulfill the need for bringing along a friend. My friend's neighbor Caroline brought someone to her first chemo, but always went by herself after that. "I felt silly bringing someone, since I went right to work afterward. I feel the same when I walk out as when I come in. Anyway, I get the chemo in a room with four recliner chairs, and we all talk to each other during the treatment. It's very social. We love our nurse, and the office manager is a delight."

PREPARING FOR THE BIG DAY

My first day at chemo I packed as if I were about to sail on the QE2. I didn't know what I might need, and I wanted to be prepared. Most chemo for breast cancer is delivered in an out-patient environment, and since hospitals and doctors are businesses and value your patronage, they will undoubtedly offer comfortable reclining chairs, pillows, and blankets. Some will also have snacks, TVs, and headphones, but don't expect a day spa.

THINGS TO DO BEFORE YOUR FIRST CHEMO

- **Visit the facility beforehand.** This gets you familiar with the terrain, a trick many people use to get over other fears, like public speaking. If you visit the physical plant beforehand, you carry a mental picture of where to go and what to expect, and a certain amount of anxiety is relieved.

- **Eat sensibly the night before.** You don't have to starve yourself, but neither should you make reservations at the all-you-can-eat buffet. You may feel queasy even before chemo simply out of nerves, and a very full stomach can make that worse.
- **Drink plenty of water.** Begin twenty-four hours earlier. It makes the veins easier to find. Continuing to drink water over the next several days will help flush out your system.
- **Pack a gym bag in advance.** This way you won't have to race around on the day of your appointment trying to choose which of twelve hundred CDs to take along.
- **Straighten up your bedroom.** This takes the edge off the nervous energy with which you'll undoubtedly be brimming. Plus a clean bedroom with a vase of flowers is a pleasure to come home to after treatment.
- **Exercise lightly.** This is also good for dispersing nervous energy, and is useful if you find yourself with lots of downtime in the waiting room. Walk around to get the blood circulating, or if you're sitting in the waiting room, squeeze the arm of your chair rhythmically to make the veins easier to find.
- **Moisturize.** Massage cream on your hands, arms, and fingertips—anywhere you might get a needle.

If you bring a book with you, now is the time for mindless fluff. You can bring your own music, either

calming or energizing as your mood suits, but people generally choose soothing stuff. You can pack a steamer
trunk full of knickknacks and distractions if you want,
but you probably won't get to use any of them (aside from
headphones). Whoever administers the chemo—your
oncologist or a chemo nurse—will usually talk to you
during the treatment, telling you what's happening step
by step, so you're not unnerved by a sudden change in
routine. You'll be asked how you feel and whether you
have any discomfort. A bit of a sedative in the IV drip is
not uncommon, so even though you might arrive at your
chemo session charged up like the bulls at Pamplona, you
could end up snoozing in your chair and surprised when
it is over so quickly.

What to Pack in Your Gym Bag

- **Something to read.** Make it uncomplicated, like fashion magazines or cheesy romance novels.
- **Something to listen to.** You may want music or guided
  relaxation tapes, depending on your mood, so bring a
  selection of tapes and CDs along with your Walkman.
- **Hand cream or moisturizer.** You won't dry out under
  the hot lights of the waiting room, but applying these
  lotions will feel comforting anyway.
- **Hobby materials.** This is a good time for knitting,
  crossword puzzles, or anything calmingly repetitive.
  You can also use the time for small, mindless tasks,
  like entering addresses into your PalmPilot.
- **Topical anesthetic.** There are prescription creams

such as EMLA you can use to anesthetize your skin before receiving a needle (see Needlephobia in chapter 6). Also bring tissues for wiping up the excess.

- **Notebook and pen.** Keeping a diary is soothing, therapeutic, and surprisingly rewarding.
- **A friend.** It's true that you can't pack this item in your gym bag. But you should bring a friend to keep you company, hold your hand, and take you home. If you're really good, your friend will schlep the gym bag for you!

BONDING WITH YOUR NURSE

The doctor devises your treatment plan, but you may find yourself spending more time with the oncology nurse who is there to see you through the side effects and the worries. "I think the nurse is the one who's nonthreatening to the patient, the one who has more time for discussion," says Maureen Major, a clinical nurse specialist at Memorial Sloan-Kettering Cancer Center. "The nurse is there to reinforce treatment, to educate the patient, and for symptom management."

Maureen Major's top three tips for new chemo patients:

- Always let the doctor or nurse know what other substances you're taking or planning to take, even if it's just a multivitamin.
- For the first forty-eight hours after treatment, make sure you eat three meals a day, but choose bland foods.
- Drink plenty of decaffeinated liquids.

DRUMROLL, PLEASE . . . THE CHEMO SESSION

The time has come. Your name is called. You trudge to the chemo area as if you were going to the electric chair. You sit. You fuss with your Walkman. You make a few pathetic attempts at humor. You look around wildly for the exit sign. It's all happening so fast.

And then it's over.

It's not over immediately, but you'll soon see that the chemo session itself is not as bad as you feared. Chemo doesn't "hurt," per se. Sometimes there is a burning sensation in the area of the IV if the chemo is pumped into the vein too quickly, but this can easily be regulated. If it burns, the person administering the chemo simply slows down the rate of infusion.

For most treatments, the actual time it takes to administer the chemo is only about twenty minutes. The rest of the time in the chair is spent with the IV pumping clear fluids to help flush out the veins.

Hospitals have an array of checks and balances to ensure that you're receiving the right chemo in the right dosage. In fact, they will probably ask for your name so many times to make sure it's really you that you'll feel like exploding. But remember, this book does not advocate violence.

The concentration or amount of chemo you get at each session is determined by your oncologist, who prescribes it initially based on body surface and other factors, and who may adjust it from one session to another according to how well your body tolerated it the last time.

These changes are incremental and you won't notice them initially.

Your body may adapt differently each session, and it occasionally happens that you'll show up for a chemo appointment with your blood count a little low. (See **Complete Blood Count.**) In such a case, chemo is postponed for a few days. During that time, you might have to give yourself injections of a **colony-stimulating factor** such as Neupogen in the thigh or buttocks. I know you are already reaching for the panic button, but stop right there! This is totally ordinary and happens to a great number of patients. The fact that your blood count is low one week does *not* necessarily mean a) the cancer has returned, b) it is time to make out a will, or c) you are the only person chemo cannot help while everyone around you is rosy-cheeked and cheery.

If you are squeamish about these injections, you can have someone else administer them for you, and although it is not the same as sharing a soda, it can be a bonding experience with your partner. Several members of my support group had times when they had to inject themselves with colony-stimulating factors, and ultimately they were more annoyed with the blip in their chemo timetable.

Although chemo may conjure terror, your sessions with it will quickly become routine, even boring. Let's backtrack a bit to when you first arrive for your appointment. You'll get a blood test to see how your blood levels are. In some centers this will be a finger prick but in others blood is drawn conventionally from the arm for testing. The first time, you probably won't have any problems, because you haven't had any chemo yet.

Next, you'll see your oncologist, who will examine you, ask you some questions about how you're doing, and set your chemo levels for that day. The doctor or nurse will probably spend a little time going over things with you, like when to take a new prescription drug or what to expect in terms of side effects or energy levels over the next few days and weeks.

Then it's probably back to the waiting room—this is where a frivolous magazine might come in handy—until the chemo is mixed and ready. They will not yell "Soup's on!" or bang a cowbell. They will call your name, you'll sit in a recliner, and the IV begins.

After your chemo, you will probably have blood drawn again, and then you will be free to go home and sleep it all off. It might behoove you to make early-morning appointments because patients start stacking up in the waiting room like planes waiting for takeoff at O'Hare.

At Memorial Sloan-Kettering Cancer Center's Breast Center, an early model for comprehensive breast-cancer care, the chemo rooms are compact units that flower off a central atrium. Each small room holds a comfortable chair, plus a visitor's chair, a rolling stool for the nurse and a counter for supplies. Many large hospitals and teaching hospitals have similar setups, or you may receive chemo in your doctor's office.

Again, you will probably not feel any of the famous, dreaded chemo side effects right there in the facility. The side effects usually kick in only after the chemo has begun to work on killing off fast-growing cells. If you feel queasy on Day One, my guess is that it is from nerves.

The doctor, oncology nurse, resident, or intern will begin your treatments with needles in the lower part of your arm, working their way up your arm as needed during future appointments. (Unless they miss the vein on the first attempt, you get one needle per visit, plus the blood-count finger stick.) You have a right to get the most experienced person for the job. After two or three unsuccessful sticks, don't be afraid to ask for someone else (it's the usual procedure in most hospitals), and don't worry about hurting feelings. Any doctor can have an off day. And a bad needle stick can "blow" a vein, rendering it inaccessible until it heals.

Chemo is usually administered in liquid form from a plastic bag that is hung on your IV or, with less caustic chemos, in a syringe. The doctor or chemo nurse squeezes the bag—it's called an "IV push"—to administer the chemo. Thus the rate at which the chemo enters the vein can easily be regulated by how hard the bag is squeezed. Sometimes an electromechanical pump controls the rate of infusion.

Chemo can be caustic stuff, and it can cause blood vessels to collapse and/or scar. Chemo can also leak from a vein. Call your doctor immediately if you notice any burning or blistering in the area where the chemo went in.

There is another way to have chemo administered that is not through the arm veins, and that is through a **vascular-access device** (VAD), marketed under such brand names as Hickman, Mediport, and Port-A-Cath. It's a small, implantable port that is surgically inserted (with local anesthesia) beneath the skin of the chest. It is attached to a **catheter** that feeds into a large vein that returns blood to the heart. With a port, there's no searching for and puncturing veins. They can just hook you up like you're at a self-serve gas station and give you all the IV fluids, antibiotics, and chemo you need. It is useful for when the treatment is highly toxic, or for patients who are afraid of needles, or whose veins are harder to find than your reading glasses when they're perched right on your nose during a senior moment. The port acts like a funnel for pouring stuff from a larger jar into a smaller one.

Despite my needlephobia, I didn't go with the port option. It has to be flushed out frequently with a blood thinner so it doesn't clot and get infected. In fact, it requires steady maintenance—periodic flushing with an anticoagulant before and after use and, with some models, every day as well. It requires out-patient surgery to insert and remove. It's expensive. Most of all, it had an "ick" factor I couldn't quite get over.

I was nervous before the first chemo treatment, naturally, since I didn't really know what to expect. My sister came home with me afterward for a sleepover, and my idea of "eating light" that night was ordering in Chinese food—a greasy wonton soup with pork. Surprise! Instant nausea. I know it's fun to blame chemo, but I think we can safely pin this one on poor judgment and rattled nerves.

3

Hair Loss

I love my hair. Did I ever curse it for not being straighter, curlier, shinier, more kempt? Did I ever treat it badly, brush it angrily, split its ends carelessly? Yes, I must admit, I did.

But I take it all back, or I would if I could. Nothing was as traumatic and mortifying during my year in Cancer World as the loss of my hair.

Whatever shortcomings I had previously ascribed to it, when it came time to part with my hair, I thought it the most glorious set of tresses that ever adorned womankind, far sturdier than Rapunzel's, more symbolic than Samson's, more lustrous than a Clairol commercial. I know at a glance how old I am in photographs because of the cut du jour, a style that changed with my changing perceptions of myself. Kindergarten, a curly, unruly mop! Sixth grade, a chic coif with a side part! College, a waist-length guy magnet!

When I have bad-hair days I feel a measurable loss of

self-esteem, and studies back me up on this. Women in particular pay as much attention to their hair as to their wardrobe, shoes, and makeup. Our hair is a big part of the image we project. And I knew that I did *not* want to project a bald image.

If only my cancer had waited a year or so. I could have been so chic. Pretty soon, Elizabeth Taylor would appear to the world totally bald after brain surgery. Demi Moore would shave her head for the movie *G.I. Jane*. How could I have known that bald women would become a fashion statement? If I had to do it all over again (and I surely hope that I don't), I would wear my baldness with impunity and look people straight in the eye. But back then, I would have put up with anything, even filling out medical-claim forms, if only I didn't have to lose my hair.

Still, no matter how bad I felt about being bald, I look back on my general cancer experience almost affectionately.

NO SHELTER FROM FALLOUT

From a technical standpoint, hair loss due to chemo is unexceptional. The chemo interferes with the ability of fast-growing cells to divide. In addition to cancer cells, other fast-growing cells are healthy ones found in the hair follicles, the reproductive organs, and the lining of the digestive tract, and the chemo doesn't know the difference—it will attack anything that dares to replicate faster than a speeding bullet. As the follicle is restrained from its normal mission, the hair shaft that was already there falls out, and a new one fails to grow in its place.

Because not every hair is in the same growth cycle at the same time, some hair falls out after one chemo session, and more hair after the next chemo session. But as soon as chemo ends, hair begins growing again like clockwork (approximately half an inch per month, just like before).

Not every kind of chemo will make your hair fall out, or at least not every kind will make *all* your hair fall out. Some will only make your hair thin, perhaps unnoticeably. Caroline Ruda, a genealogist undergoing chemo at the time of this writing, wears her long hair in a bun, and as she approaches the end of her CMF treatments, she hasn't even noticed any thinning. "All my life, I've had a comb full of hair, so I can't tell if it's any different now," she said.

If you're taking the usual dosage of doxorubicin, commonly marketed under the name Adriamycin, you're probably out of luck in the tress department. "Adria" interferes with the follicle's production of protein, which makes the hair that's already there brittle. When the hair finally makes its way to the surface of the scalp, it will break off at the brittle point.

On certain chemos, like doxorubicin and paclitaxel, your hair falls out in a very predictable way, starting mildly and then picking up speed. Your doctor or nurse can probably pinpoint the very day it will happen. Oncology nurse Maureen Major figures Day 17 or 18 to be

D-Day for hair if you've just taken doxorubicin. "Your hair may thin leading up to that, but at around seventeen days you'll experience true **alopecia**."

Even the salesman at my wig store seemed like a Ph.D. on the subject. "You're taking Adria?" he asked as we tried on different styles. "When is your first treatment? Uh-huh . . . uh-huh . . ." I thought he was about to whip out a prescription pad and a scalpel. He knew the exact timing of my hair loss.

Although most breast-cancer books don't make a big deal of this, you lose more than the hair on your head. Hair cells are hair cells, and you will notice thinning or total hair loss of the eyebrows, eyelashes, and pubic hair. This last part was quite interesting. No amount of shaving and pruning will ever give you the velvety-smooth pubis that a dose of doxorubicin can give you. Enjoy it while you can. And you can probably take a respite from shaving your legs.

Radiation for breast cancer will not cause you to lose your scalp hair again. But it may lay waste to those little curlicues around the **areola** of the nipple. You know, the ones women never admit to having. The comedian Joy Behar, currently on the ABC show *The View*, is the only person I have ever encountered who made reference to those hairs. In a stand-up routine in the early eighties, she asked women in the audience to admit they had hair around their nipples. Not a soul raised a hand.

> **Tip:** Cancer is full of indignities, and here's another one—I did not lose my underarm hair! Now, how unfair is *that*?

> **Tip:** Get a short haircut *before* you start losing any hair. The initial thinning will be less noticeable, and the cleanup easier once you begin to shed in earnest.

HOW TO SHOP FOR A WIG

Not everyone is such a princess about their hair as I was. Still, it is extremely disconcerting to wake up with handfuls of hair lying inert on the pillow. To prepare yourself both emotionally and practically for hair loss, there are steps you can take, and some of these can actually be fun.

Choose a wig *before* you lose your hair. That way you can match it to your current style and color. Unless, that is, you're one of those adventurous ones who go wild with wig possibilities—the Cher look, the Don King look, the Bride of Frankenstein look.

I went to Bitz N Pieces, a well-known wig store in Manhattan, with two friends. One was my close friend JoAnne, who visited me very often in Cancer World. The other was a mutual friend who had had breast cancer and knew the score. This other woman, we'll call her Endora, is what we refer to in my circle as "maximum," meaning one of those powerhouse women who is so focused, smart, and direct that she's scary as hell to the rest of us mere mortals. There was no dilly-dallying, no whining around Maximum Endora. Waiters don't get her order wrong. Dry cleaners don't leave spots on her fatigues. The three of us went to Bitz N Pieces and, thanks to Maximum Endora, we accomplished our wig hunt in record time.

The wig's name was Rikki (not my idea). The wig store dubbed it thus instead of giving it a serial number. The salesman had obviously been around wigs a little too long, because he referred to my wig as "she" and was appalled that I was planning to take "her" home in a plastic grocery bag. (Instead of what, a velvet-lined jewel case?) It's good to have an empathic, caring salesperson, but this guy was anthropomorphizing the wigs so much I imagine he talked to her and her wig-mates on their stands as he closed up shop every night. "Good night, Rikki! Good night, Lucy! Can't wait to comb you out tomorrow!"

When shopping for a wig, you probably want one of two things—either to replicate your current look as precisely as possible so that no one will be the wiser, or to try a look that is a departure from your normal self and will only be temporary. The second choice is more fun, but not everyone is up to the added stress of having people give your hair extra attention at a time when you may be sensitive about it.

Whichever path you choose, today's wigs are beautifully made and totally fashionable. Plenty of famous people keep wig collections so they can run out to the drugstore without having to get all dolled up for their public. Bitz N Pieces boasts many celebrity clients, and the salesman would murmur their names in my ear, as if it didn't count as name-dropping if his voice were hushed.

I woman I spoke to named Carol bought two wigs. "One was honey blonde with straight hair. My friends complained because it looked so unlike me. So I broke down and bought another one with short brown hair. But frankly, I looked better bald. My husband would ruffle my little stubble affectionately; he was so good about it."

WIG ESSENTIALS

- **Weigh your priorities.** You need to balance cost versus how natural the wig looks, because the ones that look the best are, naturally, more expensive. Wigs can be made of real hair, synthetics, or a combination.
- **Check your insurance.** Your wig may be covered by medical insurance, but you must have your doctor write a prescription that clearly describes it as a medical **prosthesis**. You can submit a receipt for only one wig, so if you buy a backup wig that looks like Carmen Miranda's fruit basket, you'll have to reach in your wallet.
- **Get precise care instructions.** The salesperson should be able to give you details for the care of your wig. Many wigs are made of real hair and need real shampoos and sets, although not with ordinary shampoo. Rinse it in cool water once a month with a mild

detergent specially formulated for wigs. Style it with a gentle touch or it will lose its shape. Don't brush it until it's dry (and dry it inside out). Specialty wig shops usually have a service that allows you to drop your wig off for a once-over the way you'd drop off your car at a gas station for a tune-up.

- **Schedule a final fitting.** Ask at your wig shop for a final fitting *after* your hair falls out. The fit will be slightly different then, and the shop can nip and tuck the wig to suit your newly streamlined scalp.

- **Get the sticky stuff.** Wigs don't stay put with just good intentions. Ask the salesperson about double-sided tape, special glue, or other adhesives they sell or recommend.

- **Provide in-between care.** A wig needs protection from dust and help keeping its shape. A wig stand is optimal, but you can improvise with a plastic soft-drink bottle.

- **Make contingency plans for sweltering weather.** Wigs are warm and can be itchy. They are especially uncomfortable during a hot flash. In the summer you may want to substitute cotton scarves.

- **Don't worry about what people think.** Wigs are made so well now that virtually no one will be able to tell you're wearing one. Men, especially. If they never noticed that you got a haircut in the old days, they certainly won't notice anything different now.

- **Shop around.** It is possible to buy wigs over the Internet or by mail order, although it's harder to guarantee the fit that way.

- **Allow room to breathe.** The feeling of security is important, but don't buy a wig so tight it cuts off circulation.

- **Keep your scalp clean and moisturized.** Remove all adhesive at night and keep the skin supple. If the skin becomes irritated, try securing the wig from a different area each day.

- **Look for privacy.** Choose a wig store that affords some privacy during try-ons. Even before you lose your own hair, you may feel self-conscious about the whole process.

Tip: Even if your insurance doesn't pay for your wig, it's tax deductible.

Tip: You don't have to spend money on a wig if you're on a tight budget. You can borrow one through the American Cancer Society.

ALTERNATIVES TO WIGS

Rikki was a noble attempt at replicating my hair, both in style and color. But I have a thing about "fakeness," and since I had been taught to think of Rikki as a person in her own right, and not just as a convenience and cover-up, I ended up never once wearing her. Instead, I wore cotton scarves that wouldn't slip, hats with oversize brims, special baseball caps (some with a fringe of bangs attached), and plain scarves in a headwrap with a contrasting oblong scarf to dress it up.

I also wore turbans. When I first thought of turbans, it was with trepidation. I imagined something Lana Turner would wear, or maybe a swami who was coaxing a snake from one in the Marrakesh marketplace. But today's turbans are lovely creations. There are plenty of specialty hat stores and mail-order venues that sell turbans and headwraps for cancer patients. Once you learn to tie the turban, it's a cinch. I went to my friend Susan Shapiro's wedding in my white-and-gold Lurex turban, danced up a storm, and no one was the wiser. The other guests probably thought that was what the well-dressed Manhattanite wears to a downtown wedding anyway.

Tip: If you're wearing a scarf, twist another scarf or two in contrasting colors into a rope and tie it around the first one like a garland, then twist and tuck the ends under.

Tip: Regular-size, store-bought baseball caps and hats do not cover enough of the head to disguise baldness completely. Ditto for regular-size scarves. Try 26- or 28-inch scarves. Longer if you're planning to do the Dance of the Seven Veils.

THE BITTER END

When your hair starts to fall out, you can (if you are so inclined) grab a clump and pull it out effortlessly. I enjoyed doing this for my friends like some ghoul out of a horror movie. It totally grossed them out and I experienced a surge of Halloweenish delight. I have written articles in the past for *Fangoria*, a magazine for fans of special-effects horror films, so my sense of humor regarding this may be different from yours.

Once the hair starts to fall in earnest, there is a phase where it looks—how shall I put this delicately?—*really bad*. Thinned clumps of hair make you look more ill than you really are, and now you can genuinely scare people—and yourself. At this point, it is advised (and it truly is better, I promise) to have your head shaved entirely. I know there's a temptation to hold on to the last shreds of your beloved hair like fetish objects at a sacrificial rite, but let's put this in perspective: it will all be back in a few months, maybe sooner. A cleanly shaved head looks a whole lot better than, as my sister liked to call it, Fright on Bald Mountain.

I asked my personal trainer, Norman, to shave my head. He was the only male to see me totally bald, but I figured that was okay, since when we were training he enjoyed seeing me grunt, sweat, and whine. He was used to seeing me look my worst, so it was no great stretch for him to see me bald.

The shave wasn't a perfect one. It remained stubbly and patchy. So it was actually a relief when the remainder of the stubble fell out and I was eligible to replace Yul Brynner in *The King and I*. Norman said my head had a very nice shape, and when you've had cancer, you want to keep those compliments coming—even the weird ones.

> **Tip:** Hair loss can hurt! But just a little. It's a strange, tingly feeling, more like pins and needles. Every follicle is alive and electric, and the feeling is slightly annoying and tender.

EYEBROW ESSENTIALS

- As your eyebrows thin, practice feathering in color with an angled eyebrow brush.
- If you lose the brow entirely, continue feathering in the area with a color that matches or is a shade lighter than your hair or wig color.
- Another method is to use two eyebrow pencils that are just a shade off each other to dot the area before feathering and softening with an eyebrow brush.
- Sometimes just the hint of an eyebrow is enough, because people tend to see an overall impression of your face without zeroing in on the details.
- Never draw a straight, harsh line even if you have an artist's steady hand. It's nearly impossible to get it perfect and it will look unnatural.
- The eyebrow begins in line with the inside of your eye. Place a pencil alongside your nose to find the starting point.

Tip: If you lose your eyelashes, you can fake it with eyeliner or a line of brown eyeshadow.

Tip: You can use fake eyelashes, but the glue may be irritating to your newly dry, sensitive skin.

IT REALLY DOES GROW BACK

The minute your chemo treatments end, or even sometimes when you switch chemo cocktails, your hair begins growing back. Within six weeks, my hair was definitely displayable again. The first time I dared remove my scarf it was summer, and I was in a diner with my friend Rita. The sweat was making the scarf sticky against the nape of my neck. "Why don't you take it off?" asked Rita, and I did, and never put it back on. Nobody seemed to notice, or maybe they thought I was a member of some political group trying to raise consciousness about baby seals.

It is commonplace for the hair to grow back the opposite of what it had been—curly if it had been straight, straight if curly. For many women, it grows back darker and/or gray, but there are aisles in the pharmacy devoted to curing just that. (You'll have to wait until treatments are finished before pouring chemicals on your head.)

There are a couple of goofy-sounding techniques that

may stem the hair loss from chemo. One is a kind of tourniquet around the forehead, another an ice pack on the head. The idea is to stop some of the chemo from getting to the hair follicles. There has been no evidence that either technique interferes with the efficacy of the chemo, but there's also no evidence that it works that well. If your hair thins anyway, sometimes it is better to just go bald.

4

❀

Other Chemo Side Effects

If you like charts and graphs, you're gonna love chemo. Well, maybe "love" is too strong a word. Among the souvenirs of my days in treatment is a chart for when to take antinausea medication during the first three days after a treatment; a calendar indicating when to take mouthwash, recipe included; and a chart showing precisely when my hair would fall out. Maureen Major, the nurse who worked in tandem with my oncologist, drew smiley faces and frowny faces on my calendar at appropriate times of the month to show me what to expect. "People love the calendars; they want me to draw a new one for them each visit," says Major. Blood counts are usually lowest a full week after chemo and last about five days, for example, but the faces grew quite happy just in time for the next treatment, when the faces would furrow all over again.

"The patient's main worry is about nausea and vomiting, which is the biggest enemy in our use of chemotherapy," says Major. "There are very good antiemetic therapies, but that's still the thing people are more concerned about." The number two worry of most patients is hair loss, followed by anxieties over nutrition, activity level, and what constitutes something serious enough to call the doctor.

Normally, I encourage readers to linger over every blessed word I write. But this is a chapter where I advise you to look up information only as needed. Your head will spin (quite unattractively, I may add) if you try to absorb too much at one time about the side effects that are possible with chemo.

I said *possible*, not likely. You may not experience any of these side effects, or you may get such mild symptoms it wouldn't even occur to you to report them—runny nose, for example, or pallid skin. Nausea, the most renowned possible side effect of chemo, is something you can actually talk yourself into, and once that is done it is easy to trigger the sensation again just by walking into the doctor's office. (That's called "anticipatory nausea" or "parking lot syndrome.")

In any case, I suggest you not read this chapter all at once, because if you never get a mouth sore then you'll never have to read or worry about the nasty things.

NAUSEA

Chemo is notorious for its primary side effect, nausea. It can set in a few hours or even a day after treatment, usually runs its course, and then subsides.

There was a time not so long ago when chemo patients

had to arrange their lives around access to a commode. But not anymore! In fact, vomiting is now considered an oddity in treatment and is reason enough to call your doctor, who will adjust your medication during your next go-round.

There are some wonderful antiemetic drugs that came into use in the early 1990s called serotonin-receptor antagonists, and they practically guarantee you won't throw up by blocking brain chemicals from triggering the gag reflex. You will undoubtedly get one of these wonder drugs administered in your IV plus a prescription for something in pill or suppository form to see you through your first few days at home. If one medication doesn't work for you, another will. My doctors and I experimented with Kytril and Compazine before settling on Zofran as the drug that had my name on it.

Another widely used drug is lorazepam, a sedative marketed under the name Ativan. This also suppresses nausea to some degree and induces temporary memory loss. (My sister refers to it as "milk of amnesia.")

You may also get a steroid in your mix. It can come in pill form, but usually you'll get it in your IV. The jury is still out on just why steroids are so effective against nausea; it's postulated that they prevent chemicals that are released by the body in response to chemo from traveling to the chemoreceptor (or chemotactic) trigger zone (**CTZ**), a portion of the brain that acts like a customer service rep. If the CTZ gets a complaint—anything from a bad smell to the sight of blood to the very thought of chemo—it announces, "Let's throw up!" Steroids help, but they come with annoying side effects of their own, like ravenous appetite and a temptation to vacuum at one in the morning.

Thanks to all these wonder drugs, I felt safe enough the night of my second chemo to go out dancing at a Russian nightclub. Far from symbolizing how tough I am, this incident just goes to show that chemo is not necessarily as bad as people think, that even when it is bad it's only temporary, and that it doesn't have to interfere with "real" life. If you choose to follow chemo with a trip to a Russian nightclub, do avoid the deep-fried pierogi.

FIRST-AID FOR NAUSEA

- **Eat lightly.** Yes to something like grilled chicken and steamed vegetables. No to the neighborhood's annual hotdog-eating competition. Proper nutrition increases circulation and makes veins easier to find.
- **Relax.** Try relaxation or breathing exercises before chemo.
- **Take drugs (the legal kind!).** Have your doctor experiment with different antiemetics in your IV until you find the one that works best for you.
- **Eat bland food.** Don't eat your favorite foods around the time you're having chemo, because you may develop an unfortunate association between the two, in which case you will never want to eat those foods again.
- **Plan ahead.** If you have a prescription for a sedative, or if your doctor plans to give you one along with your chemo, ask if you can take it twenty minutes beforehand to steady a nervous stomach.

- **Graze.** Nibble on dry cereal or crackers to absorb stomach acid.
- **Unbuckle.** Wear loose-fitting clothing.
- **Stay upright.** Don't lie down immediately after eating.

Tip: Marijuana is permitted (not only in the synthetic form of Marinol, but as your own personal crop!) for *medicinal purposes only* in eight states and the District of Columbia, as of this writing. Polls report 73 percent of Americans say they favor legalizing the medical use of pot for patients whose doctors recommend it. My doctor, spoilsport that he is, remains concerned about the acute and chronic effects of smoking unfiltered weed containing pesticides, impurities, and who-knows-what during chemo or at any other time. Some fun he is! I cannot advocate that you make illegal drug purchases in seedy neighborhoods while wearing a fake nose and mustache. But take it from me, or at least from the TV character Murphy Brown—marijuana indeed works for controlling nausea. As for marijuana's other notorious side effect, I recommend putting in an emergency supply of Mallomars.

MOUTH SORES

Mouth sores occur because the fast-growing healthy cells along the digestive tract, including the mouth, are damaged by the chemo. In addition, chemo interferes with bone-marrow production, meaning there are fewer red and white cells and platelets coursing through the blood. This can lead to, among other things, bleeding gums and bruising.

You can prevent or forestall mouth problems with good oral hygiene. But ix-nay, as they say in pig Latin, to mouthwashes with alcohol in them. This is yet another reason you're going to avoid all alcohol during your treatment. Alcohol on a sore spot in the mouth is an unpleasantly unforgettable experience, not unlike pizza burn.

How do you know when you have a mouth sore? Believe me, you'll know! But it doesn't happen out of the blue. Watch for the warning signs—reddening or white patches—and alert your doctor immediately. If it worsens, it can make eating and swallowing difficult. If you do get them they tend to go away in a few days to a week.

There are medications you can take to soothe the soreness, including a simple baking-soda rinse you can whip up at home. A half teaspoon of baking soda mixed with a half cup of water is a good everyday rinse that lowers the acidity in your mouth, especially after vomiting or eating something that stings. For more serious artillery, your doctor can call in to your pharmacy something they call "Magic Mouthwash," which is composed of equal parts lidocaine, diphenhydramine (marketed as Benadryl), and loperamide (marketed under such names as

Kaopectate and Immodium). Gargling with that can touch off the gag reflex, so I suggest you daub topically with a Q-tip on the sensitive places in your mouth. Because the preparation may numb the back of your throat, you shouldn't drink anything for half an hour afterward.

MOUTH CARE DO'S AND DON'TS

- **DO** brush your teeth with a soft-bristled brush. This is to protect the gums from tearing and bleeding.

- **DO** visit the dentist before beginning chemo. Have all the work you need done then and don't go back (unless there's an emergency) until after you're finished with chemo, not even for a cleaning. There are too many germs in the mouth to risk having them enter the bloodstream during dental work.

- **DO** keep the mucous membranes moist by sucking on hard candies or crunching ice chips. Ice chips are hard to come by outside of hospital dispensing machines, but you can make your own by wrapping a bag of cubes in a towel and hammering them. This also provides cheap anger management therapy.

- **DO NOT** eat highly spiced or acidic foods. These are foods that in normal circumstances would make your mouth tingle pleasantly. They include the obvious, like Mexican food (spices) or grapefruit juice (acid), but also the less obvious, like tomato-based pasta sauces, which can be very acidic as well.

- **DO NOT** have carbonated drinks. The bubbles can be irritating. But this is not a hard and fast rule, and if you cheat on this one, we won't tell.

- **DO NOT** eat really hot food. Let it cool off.
- **DO** eat bland food. Bland can't hurt you. It includes pasta (without tomato sauce), mashed potatoes, and other "comfort food."
- **DO** use baking soda. The baking soda and water mixture mentioned earlier is a good gargle and mouthwash. Optimally, you'd rinse with it three to five times a day, including after meals and at bedtime, beginning the day after treatment and continuing for at least two weeks.
- **DO** use the mildest setting if you're using a Water Pik.

Tip: Here's a simple rule of thumb for eating bland: Anything that would horrify you if splattered on your polished wood floors cannot be safely eaten when you are prone to mouth sores. If cola can sizzle its way through varnish, imagine what it can do when swished around a tender mouth.

Tip: The rules for mouth-sore nutrition are perfectly compatible with the rules for avoiding hot flashes and nausea. Such synergy!

INFECTION

Chemo messes with the production of blood cells in the bone marrow. With the precision of a Swiss clock, your white-cell count will dip at a certain point after chemo, making you susceptible to colds and infection. A little bug that previously would have put you in bed for a couple of days can now seriously interfere with your chemo regimen. Worse, most of the serious infections diagnosed during chemotherapy are self-inflicted. They're caused by the normal resident bugs of your mouth, rectum, or wherever. The immune system normally keeps these guys in check, but when that immune system is suppressed or not functioning optimally, the bugs get the upper hand. Whenever you feel that an infection may be developing, call your doctor. You may need antibiotics to fight it off. Hospitalization is a last resort, but it's not uncommon, so don't feel like a failure at the whole cancer-patient thing if you wind up there.

Tip: Signs of an incipient infection include fever, chills, and a sore throat.

AVOIDING INFECTION

- **Wash your hands frequently.** Do it even if you're starting to resemble the obsessive-compulsive played by Jack Nicholson in *As Good As It Gets*.
- **Wear gloves.** This is only a suggestion, not a must. You can wear a surgical mask too but people are apt to stare. They may even mistake you for Michael Jackson.
- **Don't kiss or shake hands with everyone in sight.**

Air-kiss if you must, but try graciously to avoid contact. Be direct: "Sorry, but my blood counts are low and I'm prone to infection." Or make a joke of it: "I'm in a no-kissing zone today."

- **Avoid large enclosed groups of people.** This includes the subway at rush hour, movie theaters, crowded bars (you shouldn't be drinking alcohol anyway!), or airplanes (where the recirculating air gives everyone in economy someone's cold from business class). It's a great excuse for passing on events you didn't really want to go to anyway.

- **When all else fails, act normal.** Even Howard Hughes squirreled away in his hotel room was still at risk for infection. For some people, the anxiety of monitoring their every move begins to interfere with quality of life. In that case, just behave as you usually do, and resolve to cross the bridge of infection if and when you come to it.

Tip: Most women have been brought up to please others, so it's not surprising so many of us have trouble saying "no." But if having lunch with a sneezing friend leads to two weeks of you feeling miserable, weak, demoralized, or even hospitalized, it's not worth it! One friend of mine offers a simple, "Thank you, no," and repeats it as many times as needed. Another handy fallback for cancer patients: "Sorry, doctor's orders!"

FATIGUE

It's not enough that chemo ruins production of white blood cells, which fight infection. It also lowers the red blood cell count, whose normal task is to deliver oxygen throughout the body. Neither rain nor snow nor dark of night will keep red blood cells from their appointed rounds, but chemo will cut back on service. Your energy level will therefore be lower, if you're like the 80 to 96 percent of chemo patients who experience these dips. There were times during treatment when I could have been mistaken for a three-toed sloth.

Fatigue can come at you with a one-two punch. In the second week after treatment, when your blood counts are lower and your friends have stopped fussing over you, you may start flagging. A cumulative fatigue may set in down the road. "You're much more tired at the end of the treatment regimen than at the beginning," says Major. "If you feel overwhelmed or exhausted, just rest. Otherwise there are no limitations on physical activity beyond what your body is telling you."

The danger of overdoing it lies in developing anemia, whose warning signs include fatigue, dizziness, lightheadedness, shortness of breath, difficulty staying warm, and chest pains.

Mostly, fatigue will be minor and can be accommodated with a flexible schedule. Take naps as needed, don't expect as much of yourself as you normally do, and cut down on activities that make you feel you're pushing your limits. And do mention your symptoms to your doctor. Fatigue, after many years of neglect, is now getting the respect it deserves and there's a chance your physician may have a specific treatment to offer you.

THE UNDERAPPRECIATED ART OF NAPPING

- Take naps as often as you need. It's not necessary to feel guilty or impatient with yourself.
- Regard naps as treats. Try going out of your way to make the nap a cozy, restful, and planned experience.
- Famous nappers in history include Winston Churchill and Albert Einstein, and they didn't do too badly for themselves.
- If friends have already bought you every skin-care product on the market, ask them for an "eye pillow," a gentle beanbag that rests on the eyelids to block out light for a delicious nap.
- If you have the time and inclination, get fully undressed and comfortable so you don't feel as if you're stealing a few z's.
- If you're napping in your bed, make the bed again after you've finished, or it will be a depressing sight to come back to at night.
- Nap with a friend. Or near one. I'm not kidding! Think of puppies or kittens in a basket, all curled up together. You can take a nap on one sofa while a friend is dozing off in a nearby chair.

"CHEMOPAUSE"

If you're pre-menopausal, your period may cease or get spotty during chemo because, once again, the fast-growing cells of the reproductive organs will be affected.

If you're young, this may well be temporary, and your cycle will probably return to normal after you've finished chemo. But the closer you are to menopause, the less likely it is that your period will resume. One study found that 40 percent of women under age 40 and 90 percent of women over forty are pushed into permanent menopause after chemo, although there's no way the doctors can predict what will happen in your case. I was thirty-nine when I began chemo, and my period came back even before the regimen was finished. "You have strong ovaries!" my surgeon commented, and I preened as if I had won a medal.

HOT FLASHES

Along with chemopause, you may get such menopausal symptoms as hot flashes and night sweats. They are annoying, embarrassing, and can keep you awake at night. You can cut down on their occurrence by avoiding foods that trigger them, like spices, hot liquids, and caffeine. Studies have shown that vitamin E and black cohosh may help a tiny bit, maybe by giving you one less hot flash per day, although that's not much comfort if you're getting dozens.

Hot flashes are common during menopause, and chemopause (which mimics menopause) is one of several reasons why 65 percent of breast-cancer patients experience them. Other reasons include that some women start taking tamoxifen or stop taking estrogen supplements after a breast cancer diagnosis. Tamoxifen is a synthetic hormone, a weak estrogen that occupies and blocks estrogen-receptor cells, preventing the uptake of the body's estrogen, which has been linked to breast cancer.

Recent studies have shown that some ordinary SSRI antidepressants (selective serotonin reuptake inhibitors) can help reduce symptoms. Dr. Charles Loprinzi of the Mayo Clinic has had particular success by putting his patients on the SSRI venlaxafine.

Other things to help you through the drenching:

- Wear cotton.
- Dress in layers.
- Keep a handheld fan in your purse.
- Sleep with a fan on low.
- Keep an extra cotton nightshirt handy to change into during the night.
- Stock up on specially absorbent cotton bed linens and pillow protectors (see Resources).
- Avoid stress (I know, impossible, but you can try).
- Keep an extra pillow and a bottle of water by your bed.
- Wear a cotton nightcap. I know it's goofy but it will absorb the extra moisture and keep your head warm.
- Keep a dry washcloth by the bed along with your bottle of water. You can dampen it and lay it across your forehead or neck.

Tip: Do *not* take any herbal remedies for hot flashes or other "chemopausal" symptoms without the consent of your doctor. Some remedies stimulate estrogen production, which is antithetical to your treatments.

"CHEMONESIA"

Who are you, and why are you telephoning me?

Short-term memory loss during chemo is a frequent complaint of breast-cancer patients, so much so that it is referred to as "chemonesia." This condition usually clears up after chemo has ended. Until then, try to avoid being a contestant on *Jeopardy*.

For years, women have been complaining about chemonesia—or "chemo brain," or "chemo fog"—but their complaints were dismissed as anecdotal reports. Now a few studies have confirmed what I could have told you, if only I could remember what it was I was going to tell you.

According to the *Journal of the National Cancer Institute*, a study in the Netherlands concluded that high doses of chemo for breast cancer could contribute to "memory loss and concentration lapses later in life" (although most patients receive a standard dose).

In that study, 32 percent of women receiving high-dose chemo (along with tamoxifen) sustained measurable mental impairment two years later, while 17 percent of those with the standard dose plus tamoxifen experienced problems.

These findings are similar to a Canadian study on breast-cancer patients who received chemo. As reported in the *Journal of Clinical Oncology*, a large percentage of the women in this study scored poorly on tests of memory, language, and visual-motor skills a year after treatment. Dr. Ian F. Tannock of Princess Margaret Hospital in Toronto says this can be the most devastating of chemo's side-effects.

The Canadian study also measured "mood disturbances" and found that regardless of mood, age, and education, a certain percentage of chemo patients experienced some cognitive dysfunction.

I've experienced this memory loss myself, and I can't pretend it doesn't cause me anxiety. But the fear of having "senior moments" does not justify avoiding treatment. Better to have senior moments than never to be a senior.

DEPRESSION

Show me a breast-cancer patient and I'll show you a candidate for Prozac. There was hardly a person in my support group who wasn't on an antidepressant of one kind or another.

I remember one woman in my support group sobbing because she was tired of being so depressed. Roz, the group leader, asked who in the group was taking something to help with that. Hands shot into the air, and our one depressed member dried her tears and got a prescription later that afternoon.

Cancer cells don't cause depression. But worrying about what those cancer cells are up to does. And remember—you're not alone. It's a myth that everyone but you is an exemplar of boundless optimism and good cheer. Nor is it vital that you try to be that way. If you're depressed and the depression is interfering with your daily life and ability to handle your treatments, ask for help.

CONSTIPATION AND DIARRHEA

The fast-growing cells along the digestive tract are affected by chemo, and all I can say is, keep a magazine rack in the bathroom.

Some chemo drugs are constipating. Some cause cramping and diarrhea. Go figure.

Certain chemo drugs, antiemetics, and painkillers cause constipation, which is worsened if you're getting less exercise than usual or if you're not drinking enough water. The antidote to this is to drink plenty of fluids, eat foods high in fiber, or take an over-the-counter preparation such as Metamucil. Foods high in fiber include cereal, fruit, and vegetables. Adding a sprinkling of bran to your morning cereal is an easy habit to develop.

For diarrhea, you need fluids to replace what you've lost. You can stem the tide by eating a BRAT diet: *ba*nanas, *r*ice, *a*pples, *t*ea. Gradually replace the potassium you've lost with such foods as bananas, potatoes, and apricots. Avoid extremes of temperature in your food and drink. Also avoid foods high in fiber and caffeinated drinks like coffee and tea. Most adults have at least a little trouble digesting dairy products, because they have lower levels of the digestive-tract enzyme lactase (making them lactose intolerant). When you're suffering from diarrhea, cut back on dairy products to be on the safe side.

NAGGING HUNGER

Steroids in your IV or even the chemo itself may give you the sensation that you are ravenously hungry. It may be little consolation while you're standing in front of your refrigerator to know that you're not really hungry, you're just misreading the nerve signals and the ulcerlike discomfort. Eating small, frequent meals can usually lessen those symptoms. Over-the-counter drugs such as Tagamet HB are useful for quelling heartburn, which can also be mistaken for hunger.

SPECIFIC SIDE EFFECTS OF DIFFERENT CHEMOS

With each new chemo cocktail that you receive, the doctor or nurse will give you a new set of instructions. I have a total of four blue cards—collect them all!—with different chemos listed on them, plus a handy-dandy guide to "early" and "late" side effects. For instance, nasal stuffiness and watery eyes are late side effects of 5-FU (fluorouracil), but early side effects of cyclophosphamide (marketed as Cytoxan), and since I was taking both those chemos in combination, I was sniffling coming and going.

Patients often get a mixture of chemos, like CMF or CAF. After four servings of doxorubicin, I had several months' worth of CMF, which is cyclophosphamide, methotrexate, and 5-FU. They all work in slightly different ways. For instance, cyclophosphamide interferes with the DNA of cancer cells, 5-FU with a particular enzyme, while methotrexate strips cancer cells of a vitamin they need. Sending all three in a posse at once is more likely to run the cancer cells out of town.

Here is a brief rundown of what you might expect from different chemos. It's important to remember that you won't get every textbook side effect, and even those you do get may be quite mild. I remember my nose running, for instance, but since I'm prone to allergies anyway it was not much different than a bad pollen season. All chemotherapy is likely to inspire nausea, but there are good drugs for that, so nausea is no longer Public Enemy No. 1.

- **Cyclophosphamide** (the "C" in CMF or CAF): This is the one infamous for giving you a metallic taste and bladder irritation. Sucking on mints or hard candies counteracts the metallic taste, and you have to drink, drink, drink like a fish (water, of course) for the duration of your treatments so you can flush out your system and urinate regularly.
- **Methotrexate** (the "M" in CMF): This yellowish

chemo makes you sensitive to sunlight during and even after treatment (for about a month). Use a good sunscreen. Mouth sores can develop four to seven days after treatment (see section above on combating this annoyance). As with all chemo, consult with your doctor before taking aspirin, which inhibits platelet function (it thins the blood), irritates the stomach, and masks fever. With methotrexate, you should avoid folic acid supplements, as they directly interfere with the mechanism by which methotrexate kills cancer cells.

- **5-FU** (the "F" for fluorouracil in CMF and CAF): Mouth sores and diarrhea are possibilities within a week of treatment. Sniffle alert, too. The eyes may be the window to the soul, but your nail beds and skin will reflect what's going on with 5-FU: dryness, scaly cuticles, and darkening of the nail beds may occur four to six weeks after treatment. Again, use a good sunscreen or stay out of the sun entirely. For skin dryness, don't take overlong baths, since they dry the skin even more.

- **Doxorubicin:** This very potent chemo has a range of side effects from hair loss to turning the urine red. It has the potential of doing harm to the heart and causing bronchial problems, which is why the dosage is monitored so carefully. Occasionally it causes discoloration of nail beds, soles, or palms.

- **Paclitaxel:** As with doxorubicin, paclitaxel (marketed as Taxol) produces hair loss. Bone marrow suppression, joint pain, and anemia are problems to watch out for with this drug. It can also cause mild flushing, rash, hypertension, and water retention. Some patients notice a change in taste, and diarrhea can be a problem.

WHEN TO USE THE HOTLINE

Help is available seven days a week, twenty-four hours a day, even if your doctor is off delivering a lecture in Borneo. It will make it easier during your initial visit with the doctor to take down the phone numbers of everyone you'll ever need, including the oncology nurse and the hospital. "I'm very available to patients," says oncology nurse Maureen Major, who in the days of my treatment helped me through many a crisis, from "Should I take this pill with food?" to "What does it mean when you can't sleep?"

"The most common problems patients call with are about the side effects of treatment, but also the psychosocial anxiety," says Major. "Some patients have anxiety related merely to the possibility of symptoms, and they want advice."

If you're the type of person who will break down and call only if it's truly an emergency, here are the starting guns:

- Vomiting.
- Fever greater than 100.4.
- Onset of new symptoms that were not discussed.
- Trouble eating or drinking.

THINGS TO KEEP IN MIND ABOUT
SIDE EFFECTS

- You won't get every textbook side effect. The ones you do get could very well be mild.
- During the resting period between chemo treatments, your body will develop its own pattern of recovery. You might notice that you feel worse three days after treatment, but totally fine during the third week. If you chart how you feel on a calendar, you can generally look forward to a similar schedule after successive treatments.
- No one knows it's a wig except you and all the people you blabbed to. Otherwise, no, they are not staring at you on the street.
- Side effects can be lousy, but they're not medically significant unless you require hospitalization. Schedule plenty of self-pity sessions if that's what you need to let off steam.
- Drink water. Drink water. Drink water. I mean it. It flushes out the chemicals, makes you pee, and goes a long way toward alleviating some of the side effects like nausea and bladder irritation.
- No matter how bad you think you look, everyone is going to make a fuss over you and tell you how wonderful and beautiful you are. Soak it up. You may never get so many compliments at one time again.

HOW OTHERS COPED

Carol Radsprecher, 52, painter
Treatment: lumpectomy, AC, radiation

"I had queasiness, acid reflux, and for two or three days after each chemo everything tasted like pepper, so I'd eat bland food. Sometimes I had cravings—once I wanted plum tomatoes, another time, Chinese food. But my energy level was good, and although everyone says they get tired during radiation, I felt nothing at all. Nothing! Even my skin was fine! I got through it emotionally by talking to friends—talking, talking, talking. My painting helped too. I counted down the treatments—only three left, only two left. I generally didn't feel well, but it wasn't outright awful, and I continued to work."

Caroline S. Ruda, 58, genealogist
Treatment: mastectomy, CMF, tamoxifen

"I have a great fear of nausea and vomiting, but it never happened. In fact, I was glad when my white-cell count went down and I had to take Neupogen because otherwise I wouldn't know I was on chemo. If I felt the slightest bit queasy, I took a sip of Pepsi and felt better. On days two to six after chemo I felt a little icky. I had mouth sores twice, but I swished Ulcerease in my mouth and they healed. I've had slight taste changes—I don't seem to like wine anymore—and odors bother me a lot, like strong perfume. Having chemo isn't fun, but my friends make me laugh all the time. I find so many things funny about this."

Donna Robbins, 63, eight-year survivor and hospital volunteer
Treatment: mastectomy, Adriamycin, CMF, radiation

"I remember going to get my wig and sitting there crying and angry. I didn't want to get this wig. I didn't want to have cancer. I didn't want any part of this at all. I had ups and downs, and was in the hospital with a fever for five days. Everything tasted like metal. Finally I realized I was depressed; it just hadn't occurred to me. I got a prescription for an antidepressant and it was a miracle. You shouldn't be afraid to ask for help."

Marilyn Levine, 51, sales director for a web-based company
    working with colleges
Treatment: lumpectomy, CMF, radiation

"I can't say that I feel great, because I don't. I'm tired a lot. It's that feeling of not feeling well—not horrendous, just not well. There are all these little symptoms— hot flashes, ice cold, the blankets are on, they're off. A little heartburn, a little headache, redness from one of the drugs. I work from home, so I take a rest when I need to. I haven't lost my hair but it has thinned. There was a time when I'd see one gray hair and I'd turn my calendar inside out to get my hair colored, but now it's two-tone, and I wear a lot of hats. You have choices, and I choose to say, okay, I'm going to try to stay positive, although right now after my sixth treatment I feel I've had enough of this cancer thing. Enough with this feeling not great all the time. But I look good. Some people assume because you look good you're not sick."

Teresa Moran Menendez, 59, breast cancer activist
Treatment: lumpectomy, AC, radiation

"The hardest thing to deal with was losing my hair. I had a very positive attitude otherwise. But the first time I noticed that feeling in my scalp, I pulled my hair to see whether it would fall out or not, and once it started to fall it happened overnight. In two days, I had lost all of it. That was the hardest thing. I wore a wig at the office and at social occasions, but at home, I never did. Here in Miami the weather is so uncomfortable, as soon as I got in my car I took the wig off. I was never ashamed of people seeing me bald."

Laura Kesten Merwin, 46, banker
Treatment: lumpectomy, CAF, radiation

"The day of my first treatment, my husband, John, and I trotted in with a positive attitude that this would not be as bad as I had dreaded. When I went to the commode, I giggled to see my urine come out pink. But later, that treatment left me very weak. I felt like I had slammed into a brick wall. I made a bed on the couch and this is where I stayed all day watching TV. During this time I had massive crying jags and depression. I missed my mother, who died in 1985. I felt lonely and alone. I had trouble explaining this to my husband. But my second treatment was a breeze. I had no negative side effects, took my nausea meds, and had quite a bit of energy after all was said and done. When it was time for treatment number three, I almost looked forward to it. It would mean that I was halfway done."

5

❀

Radiation, Day One

Everything I knew about radiation was gleaned from fifties sci-fi movies about lab experiments gone horribly awry. According to these movies, radiation makes you grow and grow until there are no clothes to fit you, then gives you the urge to destroy a large city.

In *The Magnetic Monster* (1953), a scientist's wayward radioactive isotope balloons until it threatens to engulf Canada. In *The Amazing Colossal Man* (1957), an army colonel who is exposed to massive doses of radiation grows to seventy feet and terrorizes Las Vegas. In *Monster from Green Hell* (1958), irradiated wasps grow too ungainly to fly, so they stomp around Africa with their tiny waists and huge stingers.

Perhaps I was misguided in my understanding of radiation. The reality is disappointingly tame by comparison. Radiation is another way of killing off fast-growing cells. The concentrated X-ray beam, discovered in 1895 by Wilhelm Roentgen, enters the cell, challenges the DNA in the cell's nucleus to a fight, delivers a few round-houses, and leaves the DNA on its knees, gasping, struggling to recover. The DNA is still trying to tell the cell to multiply and spread its dark minions, but it can barely spit out the command, so the cell, awaiting a call to action that never comes, just dies and sloughs off through the blood system, carried away like a twig on a roaring river.

Whereas chemo courses throughout your system, radiation is targeted at the area where the tumor was. A breast-cancer patient may receive between 4,400 and 5,000 rads or centiGray. The radiation is directed at the affected breast, with perhaps a concentrated boost during the last week of treatment to the tumor site. (It is concentrated only in that it is delivered to a more targeted area; it's not any different in strength than the amount of radiation you were receiving in previous sessions.) Because of the boost, you may wind up with a tan in one small area. I have such a tan, a little isosceles triangle, although it has faded with time.

If you've had a lumpectomy, you'll almost definitely receive radiation. Studies handily prove that the one-two punch of lumpectomy followed by radiation is far more effective in preventing a recurrence than lumpectomy alone. If you've had a mastectomy, you may receive radiation to the chest wall as a sort of insurance policy on the advice of your doctor.

THE SIMULATION

Radiation treatment is a pain in the, well, take your pick. Not literally a pain, because it doesn't hurt and you can't feel it. But as opposed to chemo, which is administered once every few weeks, radiation is every day, Monday through Friday, for six or seven weeks. It's time suckage, pure and simple. And it's pretty boring.

Here's my advice: as with chemo appointments, try to get the earliest possible slot in the day. I don't know what they're doing in there—oiling and polishing the machine between patients?—but the downtime in the waiting room is enormous and the backup gets worse as the day progresses. It also depends how many machines your hospital has, and how many patients are waiting for them.

After meeting with your radiation oncologist, your first appointment will be a three-hour stretch known as the "simulation." That makes it sound like the radiation oncologist has to practice in order to get it right, but it's really because the angle of the machine has to be so precise that it takes a while to fine-tune the thing. And they really do simulate the movements the machine will make during your treatments, although without delivering any X rays.

The simulation is a little uncomfortable, and I mean that in the ordinary vocabulary sense, not in the medical sense. When a nurse says you'll experience "discomfort," she probably means you're going to wish you'd never been born. But when I say the simulation is slightly uncomfortable, I mean just that. It doesn't hurt. You just have to lie still in the same position for a long time. (Don't drink a lot of liquids beforehand because there are no bathroom breaks.)

You lie on a foam or plastic mold with your arm raised over your head. If it's the foam kind, it takes an impression of your body, and when it hardens, this will be the mold you will lie in for all your treatments to make sure you're always in the same position. The more exact the position, the fewer healthy cells will get in the way of the beam. Some people take their molds home at the end of treatment as a souvenir. It's a big ol' thing and has neither cachet nor any retail value I can discern. I suppose if I become extremely famous, my fans may clamor for my radiation mold, but I really don't have the patience to store it until then.

Also during the simulation, they'll align the machine over you and make little marks or tattoos (see comments on tattoos below). They're like bookmarks so the technicians can line up the machine faster on subsequent days.

While the technicians are busy with their charts and graphs, you have nothing to do and you're not supposed to move. So far, breast cancer at least has not been dull, but this little exercise in nothingness could tax you. It's three hours of doing multiplication tables backward in your head.

It's also one of the few times in your life that a doctor will admonish you *not to lose weight*. They want you fitting that mold for the entire treatment, so you are *medically forbidden to go on a diet*! Radiation isn't looking so bad now, huh?

Oops, I spoke too soon! They may take a Polaroid of your face while you're lying there so they don't get confused and give the guy with the prostate condition your radiation plan by mistake. If they really cared about patients' rights, they wouldn't photograph any woman from this unflattering angle.

THE REAL THING

When the actual treatments begin, it's simple, but weird. You hop up on the table, fit yourself into the mold—ask for a pillow or folded towel beneath your knees, because it's easier on your lower back. (Some patients receive radiation while lying on their stomachs.) The technicians leave the room. The whole thing is done by remote control, so this big machine moves around you, stops, hums, clicks, whirrs, and moves some more. You're not entirely alone, because Big Brother is watching—the technicians can see you on a closed-circuit monitor and you can talk to them if you want. I could see one of them peering at me through a door panel occasionally. It all reminded me of the Wizard of Oz behind his little curtain.

Occasionally the machine may be out of service and the appointment will have to be canceled. I always imagined that the machine was busy that day, rented out, perhaps, the way society ladies rent the Temple of Dendur at the Metropolitan Museum of Art for charity functions. Oh, we *must* hold our next cocktail party near that darling radiation machine!

✳ INTERNAL RADIATION

There is an alternative to external-beam radiation, and that is internal radiation, where radioactive pellets are surgically implanted at the site of the tumor. For the two or three days you're in the hospital with these, you will be slightly radioactive, so your guests will have to sit on the other side of the room. However, you will not grow to seventy feet, and you will not try to destroy a large city. (If you do, please write to me and I will update this book for future editions.)

RADIATION SIDE EFFECTS

Except for the presence of large machinery, the radiation experience is sadly unexciting. You don't feel a zap, you don't turn into a zombie, you don't glow in the dark. Each session takes only a few minutes, and the rest of the time you're either jiggling your foot impatiently in the waiting room, trying to find a way to counteract the static cling on your hospital gown, or watching the technicians fool with the radiation machine, lining it up just right with your breast.

There was one thing that annoyed me greatly about my radiation treatments. The technicians sometimes rested their instruments on me while they were figuring out angles and pi and whatnot. What was I, a table? A workbench? I complained about this at my group therapy as if it were a malpractice suit in the making, and the group leader pointed out that one of our members actually worked on the same floor of the hospital. "You have a friend in Radiology," she said, and that comforted me. I was not an inanimate object! I was a person with connections at the top!

Other than the occasional bad mood, then, there are two main side effects of breast-cancer radiation to watch out for:

Lethargy: Radiation zaps both healthy and non-healthy cells. The healthy ones regenerate. But they have to work at it between sessions. Just as you are tired when your body is fighting off the flu, so you may tire during radiation. As a champion napper from way back, coming from a long line of afternoon snoozers, I hardly needed any doctor to tell me to take it easy. I believe in prophylactic napping—taking a rest even before I get tired, just in case! The lethargy of radiation fit very nicely into my normal routine. Before, there were people who made fun of me for breaking my day into two pieces. Now, it was medically mandated!

You can also feel tired during radiation if you've already been through several months of chemo. At this point, you've just about had it with the noble bearing and saintly countenance.

The bad news was that, although I felt mighty rundown by the end of radiation, I was not tired enough to skip work. Sigh.

The tiredness tends to go away a few weeks or

months after the end of treatment. Frankly, I didn't feel like myself for well over a year after the whole shebang. Some of the women in my support group reported the same, but it's hard to know how much of it was purely physical and how much was psychological. Sometimes you gear yourself up for the months of treatment and only feel the letdown afterward when you allow yourself and your body time to recuperate.

Skin changes: Skin irritations are common, more so for fair-skinned and large-breasted women. (If you're an Amazon, I guess you'll have to stock up on aloe.) The irritations generally hold off until the second or third week of treatment, and range from mild redness to a feeling of heaviness to burns that require a temporary suspension in treatment.

Toward the end of my treatment, the red, puffy, tender flesh of the radiated area began to burn. Exactly when was my burn at its worst? On New Year's Eve, thank you very much. I spent that glorious holiday swathed in a protective gel product, a kind of second skin that guards the sensitive area until it heals. I was not a happy camper. It was uncomfortable, the waterproof bandage gave off a distinctive odor, and for the few days during which I was out of commission, I felt extremely sorry for myself and bitter about the whole raw deal. A lot of my crankiness was because I was already into the twelfth month of treatment and my patience was wearing thin.

Women with larger breasts have more likelihood of getting a burn. There are extra folds of flesh for the radiation beam to pass through. On the plus side, you see it gradually redden so you can discuss the impending burn with your doctor with plenty of time to spare. Because some of the area around my lumpectomy is numb, the burn didn't hurt as much as you'd think it would to look at it. (It's pretty high on the gross-out scale, but subsides in a few days.)

My sister, who has since had surgery for endometrial cancer, was comparing scars with her childhood friend Sharon Leventon, age forty-six, who had had a lumpectomy. Sharon's scar was virtually unnoticeable, and she had no radiation burns and almost zero discomfort. "Other doctors would come to marvel at me because of this," says Sharon. "My doctors warned me of every possible side effect, but I never burned or had discoloration. I sometimes wondered if the machine was even on, because everyone expected me to burn and I didn't. In fact, I often wore my bathing suit to treatments because it was across the street from my gym and I would go swimming afterward."

RADIATION DO'S

- **DO** use common sense. You'll want to protect sensitive, reddening skin from exposure to the sun, scratches, or any kind of harsh treatment. Even a heavy shoulder bag could rub it the wrong way. If it doesn't feel quite right, then it's not good for you.
- **DO** use mild skin cleansers. The less scented they are, the better (like Alpha Keri soap). Pat dry, never rub.
- **DO** moisturize the affected area. The best time is

every night before bed, because the skin should be clean and free of residue by the time you go back for your next treatment. Only use moisturizers that have been recommended or approved by your doctor.

- **DO** wear loose tops.
- **DO** wear unstarched cotton. It's comfortable against the skin. Avoid scratchy fibers like wool or man-made fabrics like unbreathable polyester.
- **DO** use hydrogen peroxide, vitamin A and D cream, or cortisone ointments for radiation burns, but only on the recommendation of your doctor.

RADIATION DON'TS

- **DO NOT** use regular deodorant or antiperspirant. They are stinging and drying, and their components can interfere with radiation. Use cornstarch instead.
- **DO NOT** use any kind of emollient or cream on the area without asking your radiation oncologist. In any case, choose unscented lotions.
- **DO NOT** swim in chlorinated pools. (My sister's friend Sharon swam every day, but she's a rare bird.)
- **DO NOT** use your regular moisturizer on the irradiated skin without first checking with your doctor. The oils and perfumes may prove too irritating, and it may leave a residue that interferes with the radiation.
- **DO NOT** stay out in the sun. Keep the radiated area, including your back, protected from further burning. If you're wearing a sleeveless top, use UV protection on your shoulders, arms, and back. Remember, the ra-

diation goes through your body and leaves a tan on a small patch of your back as well.

- **DO NOT** take long baths. Ultimately, they will dry your skin. Also, avoid extremes of temperature when bathing.
- **DO NOT** shave or use depilatories under the arm on the side being irradiated.
- **DO NOT** wear a bra. You can wear a cotton tank or undershirt instead, with a loose overshirt. If you absolutely must wear a bra, make it a cotton sports bra or something equally comfortable. And, to paraphrase the Joan Crawford character in *Mommie Dearest*, "No underwire bras, ever!"

❋ TATTOOS

No matter where you get your treatment, the technicians will make a few small marks on your skin to delineate the boundaries of the radiation and to provide a guide for the machinery. Some hospitals will simply use Magic Marker, and if they do, you must take care not to wash or rub it off. Other facilities insist on giving permanent tattoos.

Tattoos may be all the rage among people who also dye their hair purple and want revenge on their parents, but tattoos are not for me. And have I mentioned my fear of needles lately?

Anyway, I now have seven tiny blue tattoos in a wide ring around my left breast. I had been all huffy about having to live with the marks forever and ever after treatment, but I can only locate two of them, and those with difficulty. They look like pale-blue birthmarks.

Another good reason to have permanent tattoos is to provide a guideline for future doctors, since you can't have radiation to the same area again.

OTHER POSSIBLE SIDE EFFECTS

- The radiated breast may feel different to the touch afterward. The skin may feel thicker, the breast heavier. These differences are minimized over time.
- The nipple of the radiated breast may look and feel slightly different, but if someone's looking *that* closely, they'd better buy you dinner.
- A few months after radiation, some women get myositis, an inflammation of the muscles that feels achy and goes away by itself. It is not dangerous and, no, it does not signal a recurrence.

CONCLUSION

Long-term side effects of breast-cancer radiation are uncertain and can't be predicted with any accuracy. It's a tradeoff—life and health today for unknowable possibilities in the future. I was diagnosed with asthma while I was undergoing radiation. I blame the radiation, which glanced across a portion of my lungs and heart. However, studies have shown that radiation for breast cancer does not cause heart problems, and that is indeed heartening. The asthma I can live with.

PART TWO

COPING

6

✽

Mental Strategies

There's nothing like curling up in bed with a good book. But, despite the number of excellent resources out there on breast cancer, these are not the books to be curling up with at the moment. The leader of my support group liked to say she had one rule for anyone who wanted to be in her Thursday afternoon breast-cancer support group at Memorial Sloan-Kettering Cancer Center: You had to leave your reference books at home.

Books that contain medical details can frighten as much as inform. It's important to be a well-read, educated consumer who plays an active role in her medical decisions. On the other hand, it's important to sleep at night.

Insomnia is a plague among the breast-cancer set. Some chemo causes night sweats that wake you up if for no other reason than that a rivulet of perspiration is trickling down the small of your back. I had times when my eyebrows woke me up—who knew eyebrows could sweat?

Add to this a phenomenon I call the "mind race," the tendency for your brain to whir at all times. Even when you think you feel calm, part of your mind is alive with metaphorical hand-wringing. Show me a breast-cancer patient who gets a good night's sleep without a prescription drug and I'll show you a Roswell alien that wasn't just the remnant of a crashed weather balloon.

As long as you're up, night after night, there is a tendency to kill time by poring over books and newspaper clippings, trying to find something that will shed light on your situation and help it all make sense, but scaring yourself silly in the process. The fear and sleep deprivation feed the insomnia and other side effects. All this can be soothed with mental strategies.

One of the keys to a happy life is to accept that there will inevitably be obstacles, and while you can't necessarily predict or avoid them, you can do your best to make peace with them. One day when you are in a better mood about all this, you may realize that dealing with life's obstacles is part of the exciting challenge of being human. It can be embraced as an adventure.

Thus begins the adventure of coping with breast-cancer treatments.

INFORMATION OVERLOAD

What's a girl to do when she can't sleep? I, for one, amused myself by dragging huge medical compendiums into bed and staying up all night reading about what undoubtedly would be my own terrible end. Although my diagnosis had been invasive **ductal carcinoma**, a common type of breast-cancer tumor, I trembled with a terrible excitement over textbook chapters on rare cases and conditions that I decided I probably also had. The doctors may have missed it, but I was on the case every night at 3 A.M.

If it was a particularly long night, I might have time for the *Merck Manual* as well, where I could read up on other illnesses I didn't have and probably never would. Never underestimate the zeal of a sleep-deprived imagination.

Cancer patients are already jumpy. You'd think we wouldn't want to make things any worse for ourselves. But fascination overcomes discomfort. There was a time not so long ago when cancer patients weren't even told what they had so as not to alarm them, but I was quite up to the minute. I examined the statistics, usually concluding that my days were numbered by ever larger factors. I found inventive new ways of interpreting reams of data to prove that my goose was cooked. Charred, really.

I can assure you that I didn't think of it as self-torture. The most fundamental panic during a cancer diagnosis is the feeling of loss of control. We suddenly realize that control is an illusion. You can exercise, eat right, get eight hours, and still get hit by a bus. The tough truth is that you can only do your best while fate, genes, random events, dumb luck, and the natural deterioration of the body over time all take you in unexpected directions, no matter how many protein shakes you drink or how many times you call the Psychic Friends Network.

So it's understandable that some breast-cancer patients seek information—about their cancer and about other health factors, like nutrition—as a way of regaining a sense of control over their lives. (Breast-cancer patients tend to hang out in the healthy-eating section of the library.) Knowledge is power, but information overload is not productive, and some information is downright unhelpful.

Statistics, for example. Statistics speak in bell curves and generalities of populations, which says nothing about you as an individual. Even the famous "one in eight" statistic is misleading. I like it because it galvanizes fundraising campaigns and heightens awareness, but the figure is based on a population living a very long time. If you live to be ninety-five, you will have a one in eight chance of getting breast cancer. At that age, you'll probably have a one in eight chance of remembering what you ate for breakfast, but them's the breaks when you're pushing a hundred.

We have this one-in-eight figure because advances in science and medicine have enabled the population to live that long. And the longer you live, the more chance that you'll get *something*.

Still, I wanted to know—where did I fall on this continuum? With my diagnosis, there was a 60 percent chance I would have a recurrence within five years. So, was I going to be in the 60 percent camp or the 40 percent camp? Just to be on the safe side, I decided without any medical input that I was in the 60 percent camp—just my luck! Is the glass half full or half empty? Why, it's bone dry!

When you're tired and obsessed and worried, you can go nuts with information, until it is no longer information—that is, facts that lend clarity to a situation. So here is my advice, from someone who already screwed it up: keep a stack of inconsequential magazines by the side of your bed for those late nights, and if you must get your fill of information in the wee hours, let it be on fashion secrets and the problems of millionaire celebrities.

There are people who go in the opposite direction as well. Some patients don't want to know a thing about their illness. It's like that scene in *A Few Good Men* where Jack Nicholson explodes on the witness stand: "The truth? *You can't handle the truth!*" Some people just don't want to know anything that might disturb their equanimity.

Might I suggest a moderate balance (not that I've ever been able to achieve such a thing myself)? You need a certain amount of information in order to make informed decisions about your treatment and to understand what is "normal" and expected. But you should avoid overburdening yourself with speculative information about what might or could happen to you or someone like you in a parallel universe.

WAYS TO FILTER INFORMATION

- **Delegate.** Have someone else, maybe the bookworm in the family, digest information for you and brief you like a busy politician. My sister read a lot of cancer books and distilled information for me on a need-to-know basis.
- **Apply limits.** Medical information is like caffeine—it stays in the system for several hours. So make it a policy not to terrify yourself after, say, 4 P.M.
- **Avoid junk.** Don't buy books or listen to people who make broad, unsubstantiated, and frankly weird claims about curing cancer with thought waves, foods grown during a full moon, or strange supplements known only to the ancients and a few people on the Internet.
- **Use discretion.** Look up specific symptoms only as you experience them. Don't anticipate what hasn't happened yet.

KEEPING YOUR FOCUS

Looking for something certain and immutable to latch on to is one of the great recurring themes of a cancer diagnosis. Related to that is a tendency to focus on a small aspect of breast cancer rather than on the whole mind-boggling thing. That is why you may find yourself seemingly not bothered at all by breast cancer, but totally obsessed with how awful it is that your nail beds have darkened (as they can with doxorubicin).

When you find yourself becoming obsessed with

things that are trivial by comparison—a temporary drop in your blood count, a sudden disruption in your schedule—it is often just a healthy coping mechanism that gives you temporary relief from looking at the big picture. If you'd like to take more control of this and remove your thoughts from the cancer sphere altogether, you can further redirect your thoughts to more positive subjects—not because positive thinking will cure cancer but because it can, in fact, relieve a stomachache, regulate breathing, reduce adrenaline flow, relax the muscles, and just plain make you feel better.

You don't have to be a Sufi on the mount to know the secret of redirecting your focus. It's actually quite easy:

- **Keep lists.** On a piece of paper or on your PalmPilot, keep handy a short list of topics that interest and involve you (like gardening), but don't make you crazy (like JFK conspiracy theories). Choose one to dwell on for ten to fifteen minutes at a time. Examples: identify birds, or envision a new filing system for your important papers, or map out the perfect garden, or mentally catalog examples of your pet's body language.
- **Retrace your steps.** Think of how you accomplished something physical or mechanical that was challenging and brought you pleasure—the steps by which you improved your swim stroke, for example, or how you fixed that computer crash, or baked that cake from scratch.

- **Remembrance of things past.** This is for the Proust lovers out there. Close your eyes and imagine your childhood bedroom. Visit it in your mind without skipping any details—the position of the furniture, the texture of the bedspread, the clippings on your bulletin board, the toys on the shelf.
- **Back to the future.** Refine your favorite fantasy—accepting the Nobel Prize, for example. It's okay, no one's looking.
- **Repeat a mantra.** Champion meditators often use a private word or phrase, like "Om" or "Breathe," which they chant in their heads while clearing their minds of everything else.

NEEDLEPHOBIA

If you're going to have chemo, you're going to have needles. But believe me when I say that if I could get through it, so can anyone.

I have yet to meet a person who actually likes needles. (Oops, I take that back. My research assistant, Ramy, says she likes needles, but I think she's messing with me.) Nevertheless, there is a gulf that separates me, a certified lifelong needlephobe, from those who merely detest them. Needles make me whimper, faint, and otherwise act like an idiot. My needlephobia is not a pretty sight.

An extreme fear of needles is what is known as a "simple phobia" or "specific phobia," a "marked and persistent fear of clearly discernible, circumscribed objects or situations," according to the *Diagnostic and Statistical Manual of Mental Disorders*. A simple phobia can be a fear of rottweilers or porkpie hats, if you're so inclined. Apparently, only 9 percent of the population suffers from simple phobia, and of those, only 20 percent ever get over it. I am one of the lucky 20 percent, although it took a lot of work, and even now I shift uncomfortably in my seat whenever there are injection scenes in movies.

It all stems from a childhood trauma when an inexperienced nurse got a needle stuck in my arm. She twisted and turned it while saying such confidence-building things as, "I dunno, I just can't get it out!"

When I was younger, it was probably cute when I'd faint during a blood test, like a tender maiden from the days of yore. Lately, the effect has not been quite as adorable. The last time it happened, I gradually awakened to discover I was slumped in my chair, moaning to wake the dead, and drooling just a tad. All this in front of one of those handsome doctors, the kind whose left ring finger you sneak a peek at.

My needle peccadillo and I were getting by just fine, with the occasional dark interlude known as the Annual Checkup, when I discovered I was in for nine months of chemotherapy. Imagine my surprise.

I was referred to Dr. Steven Passik, a behavioral psychotherapist who is now director of oncology symptom control research at Community Cancer Care Inc. in Indiana. Most people who come to Dr. Passik are depressed or anxious about their illnesses. "They are struggling to adjust to their disease, and they're anxious and fearful about the future," he explains. "Even people who have simple phobias that don't generalize to a gazillion other circumstances can usually go through life avoiding the one thing that makes them freak out. But in your case, you had to deal with it."

During an interview with Dr. Passik for this book, I made him swear that mine wasn't the worst case he'd ever come across.

"Well, I guess you could say technically that it's true, because there are some people who actually forego their medical treatment because their fears are so severe," replied Dr. Passik, who is accustomed to humoring me.

There's a three-pronged approach for treating people with fear of needles (or fear of anything, for that matter): "Desensitizing the patient to the stimulus, breaking down the avoidance, and containing the panic in the face of it." And there are two ways to accomplish those three things: gradually or in a process called "flooding," which is the sink-or-swim approach.

To desensitize the patient, says Dr. Passik, "you take a stimulus that used to invoke tremendous panic, and begin the process of separating from that, or substituting for the panic. I teach the person how to go into a deep state of relaxation, then have them imagine the stimulus, teaching them to maintain the relaxation during the thought of the stimulus. In this way, you can construct a hierarchy of fears, where item number nine or ten might be the actual stimulus."

To break down the avoidance, you gradually reintroduce the object of terror into your life until you build up more of a tolerance to it, like creating mental antibodies to the source of fear. For instance, you can practice meditating and imagine being near a needle but not in contact with it. If you imagine this often enough, you will no longer be so panicky. Then you can progress along Dr. Passik's "hierarchy of fears" until you are coping with the thought of the injection itself.

Dr. Passik gave me so many tips and exercises that I was still unpacking the arsenal when it was time to go home. The idea, ultimately, is to "contain the panic," and Dr. Passik had a lot of tricks up his sleeve for that.

- **Don't look.** Do not peek at the instrument of torture. It will only press the panic button in your head.
- **But keep your eyes open.** Remember that childhood trick where you close your eyes and your friend puts an ice cube on your arm, claiming it's a lit match, and you jump with pain? With your eyes closed, it's hard to tell just what sensation your brain is processing. And just as in childhood, bugbears loom larger in the dark. With eyes open, there is more sensory input to distract from frightening imagery.
- **Chat.** If you can't keep up your end of a conversation, just let others babble to you. It's an excellent distraction.
- **Visualize pleasant things.** Dr. Passik recorded a guided visualization tape for me in which I was back at the bungalow colony of my childhood summers in Pennsylvania. This tape was infinitely longer than

the time it took to find a vein, so by the time I was imagining being reunited with my dear departed hamster,* the deed was done. When you're visualizing something you like, pay close attention to detail—how the ground feels beneath your feet, perfumes in the air, the sound of birds, the way your hamster hid in your shirt pocket, etc.

- **Breathe.** Take long, deep, steady breaths, in through the nose and out through the mouth. They teach this kind of breathing in yoga, relaxation, and stretching classes, and there's nothing secret about it—it refreshes the body with oxygen, distracts you from the thing at hand, and prevents the shallow panting that leads to hyperventilation and fainting.

- **Topical anesthetic:** A prescription cream such as EMLA is a little unwieldy to apply but it dulls the nerve endings on the skin so you don't feel the needle as much. No one ever told you about this cream, huh? It works like a charm. It is now used routinely in pediatrics so that the children of today won't think of injections as horrific events. The problem with such creams is that they're messy. You have to apply it about half an hour before the needle prick, then keep the area covered with plastic wrap. There are a few drawbacks—the chemo goes into whichever vein looks most accessible that day, and it may not be the one you lovingly slathered in goo. There is also the very real possibility that your plastic wrap will unravel

---

*Just so you know, Laura Merwin, a breast-cancer survivor who is quoted in this book, is the one who gave me and my sister Cleopatra the hamster.

and leave a greasy trail of cream on whatever magazine you're reading, plus on your clothes and Walkman. In addition, I guarantee that you will be ridiculed mercilessly by anyone who sees you performing this little routine in the waiting room.

- **Sedatives.** This is something to discuss with your doctor, but mild sedatives are quite commonly prescribed to help the nervous, the very nervous, and those of us who are ready for the padded cell. A little something from the benzodiazapine family, such as Valium, Ativan, Xanax, or Clonapine, can help calm you down before chemo. "Ativan is good because of its known property of retrograde amnesia," says Dr. Passik, "so it's not only a sedative, but people really do not remember the whole episode later."

Dr. Passik would not have presumed to rob me of my phobia, as distinctive as a birthmark. I still proudly call myself a needlephobe and gather people around the campfire to hear the story of the bad, bad nurse who instilled it in me. Still, long after chemo is over, I can get blood drawn with the best of 'em.

A postscript: At my very last blood test, I decided that for the first time in my life I would actually look at the needle. Watching didn't kill or traumatize me after all. The needle was embarrassingly tinier than I had imagined it, and the procedure looked quite interesting, all things considered.

DUMP YOUR TOXIC FRIENDS

The rule regarding relationships and cancer is that good friends get better and bad ones go *phfffft*. (That, by the way, is the technical terminology.) So while my other friendships grew stronger than adductor muscles on a Thighmaster, things between me and one of my friends—we'll call her Murgatroyd—got so bad we ended up never speaking again. To use cancer terminology, our split did not leave clean margins.

Murgatroyd was a hypochondriac who was always making her dramatic farewells to the world whenever she sneezed. It wasn't the only problem between us, of course. But Murg actually seemed jealous—in one of those weird, attention-grabbing ways—that her little aches and pains couldn't compare to my glorious burst of cancer. She had worn people down over the years, squeezing them for sympathy over imagined or exaggerated ailments, only to see me run off in the end with the flower arrangements and Kiehls gift baskets.

I was a reluctant entrant into this contest over who had the most to lose. With cancer, I could no longer sympathize with Murg's headaches (brain cancer!) and stiff necks (bone cancer!). She could have the flowers if she wanted. (The Kiehls products I was keeping.)

It turns out that the next best thing for a hypochondriac who hasn't had any good symptoms lately is to be the best friend of someone who does. Murg established herself as the point person for my illness, the one who gravely related my condition to others. She reveled in the reflected glory of dire statistics, bravely fighting back tears when describing my uncertain future. Leave it to Murg that I get cancer and she makes it all about her.

Murg continued to suffer visibly on my behalf even though she didn't seem to think much of me and totally ignored my primary and desperate wish to stop our wearying all-night phone calls.

For a while, I struck a delicate balance with sleep. Then, one night, Murg kept me up on the phone until *six in the morning* trying to hash out something she didn't like about me. When you're going through treatment, you're at your most vulnerable, and I didn't feel strong and secure enough to simply hang up on her. I made vague noises about how late it was, how this conversation could wait, but she was still operating on all cylinders and wouldn't let me go.

That phone call pushed me over the edge. I was outraged that she could be so cruel as to wear me down physically and emotionally at a time like that. I stopped speaking to Murg. Not an elegant solution, I'll admit. But then, neither is chemo; yet it works.

My experience with Murg is typical in many ways. Most of us have a few toxic friends cluttering up the social landscape. Worse than that, sometimes the toxic person in your life is a family member, someone who'll always be a blood relative and simultaneously a pain in the behind.

Toxic friends and family sap you of your energy, make you feel ill, and don't have your best interests at heart (although they swear very loudly that they do). You might stick with them out of guilt, or habit, or spinelessness, but it's not until cancer forces you to make tough choices on so many fronts that you may feel the strength and motivation to clean house.

A cancer diagnosis makes you more alert than a grande espresso at Starbucks. You quickly size up who is in your corner and who, as they say in Yiddish, "*hoch mir a chinik*," which literally means "rattle me like a teakettle."

Dump the toxic friends and put strict limits on toxic family members. Do it now. Get them out of your hair (or your turban, or your store-bought rasta braids). Remember, when it comes to toxicity, at least you can be sure that chemo eventually leaves the system, whereas some people produce side effects like depression, anxiety, irritability, and sleeplessness forever and a day. Funny how you never really noticed that before cancer clued you in.

FRIENDS ARE TOXIC IF . . .

- They keep you on the phone all night.
- No matter what you're discussing, they find a way to upset you.
- You need more than two Rolaids after they visit.
- Your neck is so tense after seeing them, even a shiatsu therapist who walks on your back can't work out the kinks.
- Upon seeing them you think, "Oh no, here we go again!"
- They respond to your illness with stories of people who had it worse.

How to Neutralize Toxic Friends (and Family)

- **Delegate.** Establish a "point person" for updates on your health and have everyone else go through that person for information.
- **Pass the buck.** "I'm sorry but I have to limit my socializing for the next few months, doctor's orders."
- **Play the cancer card.** "My illness has forced me to reassess some things in my life, and right now I need some time to myself so I can concentrate on getting well. I really need some time alone right now and I hope you will respect that."
- **Be blunt.** No one will be mad at you while you have cancer. "When you're negative like that, it's not helpful to me. And I really need you to be helpful right now," or, "Please let's save that conversation for a time when I have the strength to handle it."

✳ SHOPAHOLISM

There's one side effect of breast-cancer treatment that has not been studied, but I'm here to report from personal experience and observation that it is a pervasive syndrome. It's shopaholism. One in eight women gets breast cancer, but ten out of ten breast-cancer patients overspend. Just as you shouldn't operate heavy machinery after taking a sedative, a woman who is battling breast cancer should not be allowed anywhere near her credit cards.

I'm not saying this just because I myself ran up incredible tabs, which I am still paying off to this very day. At meetings of my support group, there was hardly enough room for the participants with all the shopping bags they hauled in from Saks and Bergdorfs. In a pinch, if we were pressed for time, we'd run into the Breast Center boutique and buy a couple of scarves or pink-ribbon pins, so desperate were we to quell our anxiety by buying presents for ourselves. The first ten minutes of each meeting were spent rustling about in tissue paper and admiring each other's stress purchases—clothing, jewelry, maybe some sample tiles for a new kitchen counter.

Did you know that a high percentage of breast-cancer patients remodel their kitchens? I know I did. One woman had a new bookcase made to order. Another lugged home a 27-inch TV. A close friend had a biopsy which proved benign, but she went out the day of the procedure and traded up to a new sports car anyway. I'd hate to see what she'd buy if she were in real trouble.

You're probably thinking we were all rich to begin with. Not! Most of us were in the ordinary earnings brackets, but our powers of rationalizing were without limit: I deserve a little something! I needed this anyway! A new kitchen will increase the value of my home! If it makes me feel good, why not?

And, my favorite: It's Thursday! (Or Tuesday, etc.)

I decided right after my treatments to renovate my entire apartment. The pièce de résistance was the bathroom, with a Jacuzzi, limestone tiles, and gleaming surfaces. I figured that if I ever had to spend a lot of time feeling nauseous again, better to have cool tile to rest my head against. Now I have a bathroom I'd be proud to be sick in.

If shopaholism is getting you down, or if you don't want to receive chemo within the dank confines of debtors' prison (so unsanitary!), here are some tips for kicking the habit:

- Cut up your credit cards.
- Window-shop, don't buy.
- Give me everything you've bought; that'll teach you.
- Get a grip.

- Distract yourself with a phone call.
- Carry a list of your collectibles so that you don't mistakenly buy duplicates.
- I know you feel like it's now or never, but believe me, you're going to live to spend another day.
- Steer clear of Internet impulse purchases.
- Imagine a life beyond cancer, one in which you have to pay off these bills.
- Be kind to yourself so that you don't feel an overall sense of deprivation.
- Reward yourself as you would a child, with small, inexpensive treats.

ROCKING INSOMNIA TO SLEEP

Breast-cancer patients don't sleep well, not even with soft sheets, an electronic sound soother, hot baths, and slow sheep. If you want to find breast-cancer patients, check the Internet chat rooms at two in the morning.

It's hard to relax enough to fall asleep when your mind is racing a mile a minute with Very Bad Thoughts. And who can fall asleep if you're still tallying up whether you lived this day as if it were your last, grabbed for the gusto, enjoyed life to the hilt?

Also, some types of chemo induce menopausal symptoms, which include the aforementioned night sweats, which tickle while they trickle.

Meanwhile, it's very important to be well rested so

that your body can cope with treatment. The goal is not to find some way to get by on less sleep, but to find a way to get a good night's rest.

A quick and easy way is with a prescription from your doctor for a sleeping pill. There are some very gentle ones out there that don't leave a "hangover" or give you nightmares. Yes, they can be habit-forming, but it's not like you're going to turn into a heroin addict robbing people in the streets for your next fix. It's just that once you start taking it, it's eventually hard to get to sleep without it. I was annoyed at being so dependent on so many drugs—chemo, antiemetics, sleeping pills—but each one served a purpose whose benefits outweighed the risks. Sleep deprivation can make you more susceptible to infections and colds, and with your low blood cell count during chemo these conditions can blossom into causes for hospitalization and delays in treatment.

Whether or not you resort to medication, there are plenty of things you can do to help yourself deal with chronic insomnia.

DRIFTING OFF THE NATURAL WAY

- **Your bed is for sleeping.** If you're wide awake, move to a different spot, like a chair, and read for fifteen minutes, then get back in bed and try again to fall asleep. Repeat this exercise as often as needed.
- **Your bed is an exclusive haven.** Plump the pillows, fluff the comforter, change and smooth the sheets, don't use your bed to sort the laundry. Comfort is key.

Don't be afraid to make your bed look like an oasis out of a romance novel if it helps you snuggle in luxuriously at night. Insomniacs come to think of their beds with anxiety. Counteract that by making the bed a place you love to nestle in even if you don't fall asleep.

- **Keep a fan on low.** It will keep the air circulating and cool you in case of night sweats.

- **Take a warm, not hot, bath.** Follow up with a body moisturizer (unscented in case you have an aversion to certain odors).

- **Sip something warm and soothing.** The standbys are hot milk, cocoa (although that contains caffeine), and herbal tea. The teas with pictures on their boxes of teddy bears dozing in rocking chairs are the ones that will help you sleep. Avoid the ones that have "zinger" in the title.

- **No exercise, caffeine, or food at *least* two hours before bed.** Actually, don't have any caffeine at all past 4 P.M., and remember that colas and chocolate contain caffeine as well.

- **Listen to music that is soothing or has a narrative.** Don't laugh—I listened to *Peter and the Wolf*. You get sleepy just following along semialert.

- **Do relaxation exercises in bed.** You may not realize until you concentrate that you have been clenching your neck muscles like the Romanian weightlifting team. Relax by first tensing every single muscle in your body, then concentrate on releasing each one slowly, starting at the toes and working up to your eyelids and forehead.

- **Think kind, gentle thoughts.** Do not let your mind stray toward what you coulda-shoulda said to some jerk in the parking lot. Bad thoughts cause your body to tense and pump adrenaline, which is anathema to falling asleep. There will be time enough to worry about these things tomorrow. Needless to say, now is not the time to balance your checkbook in your head.
- **Do something quiet or methodical before going to bed.** Reading or indulging in a skin-care routine are obvious choices.
- **Don't nap.** True, I spent most of this book extolling the pleasures of napping. But when it interferes with your nightly rest then try to go without naps for a few days until you're back on schedule.
- **Don't try herbal remedies without your doctor's advice.** If you are thinking of using valerian root or other supposed soporifics, first make sure they won't interfere with the particulars of your treatment.

ENEMIES OF SLEEP

- Your mind is in overdrive
- Side effects of various medications
- Growing dependence on sleeping pills
- Night sweats
- Nausea or "blah" feeling
- Anxiety about the future

RECOMMENDED BEDTIME AMUSEMENTS

- Celebrity gossip magazines
- Visually oriented magazines, like *Architectural Digest* or *Vogue*
- Dryly informative magazines, like *Consumer Reports*
- Nature books with pictures
- Favorite storybooks from childhood, like *Anne of Green Gables*
- Travelogues
- Humor books or audiotapes
- CDs of nature sounds or bird calls
- Guided meditation tapes

FORBIDDEN AT BEDTIME!

- The *Merck Manual*
- Other people's cancer memoirs
- Your medical chart
- Conspiracy theories about how the government is spying on you or how big business is poisoning you
- *Mein Kampf*
- Books about biological terrorism and emerging viruses
- Yoko Ono CDs

UNNECESSARY BUT GRATIFYING SPENDING OPPORTUNITIES TO HELP YOU SLEEP

- Bubble bath. If you're undergoing radiation, don't immerse yourself totally or the lotion may irritate your breast.
- Two cozy sleep-shirts. Keep one handy in case you get drenched with night sweats.
- Bathrobe. Treat yourself to the waffle-weave absorbent kind.
- Headphones. Spring for the ultra-padded ones.
- New bedding. The higher the thread count, the better. Go Egyptian!

Tip for Limiting Phone Calls: Change the outgoing message on your answering machine to give times of day when you're available to call people back. This way you can screen your calls and limit the time you spend on the phone without feeling guilty.

Tip for Streamlining Updates: If you're Web savvy, set up a Web page (or have a friend do it) with updates on your treatment so that you don't have to repeat the most recent news a million times. Give the URL to friends so they can log on and leave you messages.

WORDS OF WISDOM FROM
OTHER SURVIVORS

"You'll get through it. It's doable. It may not seem that way right now, but it is." — Carol Radsprecher

"You muddle through, day by day. At first it's like walking through mud. After a while, it's like walking in sand, still not smooth, but better. Then you hit grass, and you're home free. So you have to realize you take some time out because you're going through an illness, but it's going to get better, and you have to handle it on a day-to-day basis." — Donna Robbins

"I know it's awful, but you have to accept the fact that you have breast cancer, and decide—I'm not going to be ashamed of this. I'm a woman, and this happens. You say, I'm going through this, and I'm going to get through this." — Marilyn Levine

SAY IT WITH GUSTO

The first time my mother said aloud that her daughter had cancer was at a family meeting at Gilda's Club. Before becoming a member of this supportive, relaxing retreat, named after the late Gilda Radner, it is required that you attend an introductory group session where you're invited to bring along one or more family members. We went around the room introducing ourselves and saying a bit about why we were there.

"I'm here with my daughter, who has breast cancer," said my mother, starting to cry. "This is the first time I've said it out loud."

People of my mother's generation didn't say the word "cancer," maybe not even to themselves. Cancer was too fearsome and stigmatized a thing to be acknowledged.

"Forty years ago we called it The Big C," says Roz Kleban, an administrative supervisor in the Department of Social Work at Memorial Sloan-Kettering Cancer Center. "The best way to deal with the cancer is to wrestle with it and talk about it. Pushing it away enhances and reinforces it, making it a big ugly thing you're afraid to look at. Talk about it, jump on it, hold it, examine it, and you'll see it's not as scary as a thing you can't pronounce. The movement to say the word 'cancer' gives you the idea that, hey, this is something I can deal with. Public figures are getting up and saying, 'I have cancer.' The person who is terrified but saying it out loud is helping herself. The old way of repressing it doesn't work out as well; then you take it with you forever."

I had difficulty myself in saying the word "cancer" at first. But I quickly got the hang of it. I tried to use "cancer" in conversation as much as possible. I made jokes about it. I said it forthrightly, even if it made other people flinch. I was determined that this word not have any power over me, no power to make me ashamed or uncomfortable. I work with words for a living, and by golly, you have to whip those buggers into shape!

And so I am not afraid of the word "cancer." It is part of my normal vocabulary. And I have incontestible support for my method from no less an authority than *Harry Potter and the Sorceror's Stone*, when the child sorceror is told he doesn't have to call his nemesis You-Know-Who anymore: "Call him Voldemort, Harry. Always use the proper name for things. Fear of a name increases fear of the thing itself."

7

Getting the Support You Need

One of my happiest experiences during treatment was going to my Thursday afternoon breast-cancer support group. Women dropped in and out of the group as time went by, but we had a core of a dozen who began treatment around the same time, so it felt as if we were going through the experience together. For years after we stopped needing the regular meetings, group members still met informally for lunch every few months.

Forming strong human connections helps people live longer. Think of the babies in orphanages who die if they are deprived of the simple reassurance of the human touch. Think of the hapless men who fall apart after a divorce, probably because there is no one to throw out their pizza boxes for them.

Barbra Streisand said it best when she said, "Photograph me from my good side." Just kidding. People need people, and when in crisis, people need personal support more than ever. Interdependent relationships, whether with spouses or friends, are crucial for human survival in ways that science is only beginning to comprehend.

Breast-cancer support groups are numerous, and can be found through local hospitals and national organizations. Women in breast-cancer support groups discuss how to deal with all aspects of the illness, including tough subjects like taking an active role in your health care and demanding the service and attention you need. The groups provide many different sources of information sharing. I spotted the incomparable Linda B. pass another woman a tube of Astro-Glide. Another member once removed her prosthesis and bounced it across the table so that the curious could get a closer look. Mostly we comported ourselves with dignity, but there was that day when several women removed their wigs and twirled them like caps at graduation.

Roz Kleban of Memorial Sloan-Kettering Cancer Center has worked with oncology patients for nearly twenty years, specializing in breast-cancer patients in the last dozen years. She ran the Thursday afternoon support group, and of all the people in white coats I had to deal with during Cancer Year, Roz was my favorite. She has a very down-to-earth attitude, and now that I have the benefit of twenty-twenty hindsight, I can see the subtle and gentle ways she tried to steer me and the group away from mental harm.

"There are tremendous similarities in the ways people respond to major disease," she says. "But there are issues that pertain to some illnesses in greater detail. With breast cancer, there are physical appearance, sexuality, and fertility issues. I see about a thousand breast-cancer patients a year, so I can bring consensus and validation to them."

Kleban sees patients individually as well, but she says the group approach is probably the most helpful intervention.

There are other aspects of the group that pertain to being all-female. (If you are among the 1 percent of breast-cancer patients who is male, I apologize once again for leaving you in the dust.) "When people get an illness, many of their roles are taken away from them," notes Kleban. "You're no longer car-pooling or being the care-givers you usually are. You lose these roles temporarily. In a group, you are given back the ability to take care of others. When you join a group in the beginning, you are frightened. Later, you initiate other people. There's a sharing of information. Nothing reduces anxiety as much as knowledge."

The group is not forever. People continue to attend as long as they feel they need it. Kleban figures the average is nine months, which covers their time in chemo and/or radiation and a few sessions to cope with separation anxiety. Carol Radsprecher was still attending her group nearly a year after she finished treatments. "I feel a real closeness with the other women," she explained. "They're very intelligent, and there's closeness even though the members of the group change as time passes. The best part of the whole breast-cancer experience was meeting these women, without sounding too corny about it. When I first joined the group, I was a little nervous. Sometimes I cry when other women tell their stories, but mostly we laugh, giggle, have a good time. I'm an atheist, and this is my church."

Everyone outgrows the group eventually. "During the group, people are just struggling to get through things," says Kleban. "There are very pertinent issues for someone with adjuvant treatment. There's fear of treatment, coping with going back to work, coping with friends and relatives, coping with hair loss. There are hundreds of issues—the meaning of cancer, how you think you look to the rest of the world, the difference between reality and your perception. You can't just come to eight sessions and say you have it under your belt. There's a constant rehashing and working through of these issues. The person who has been there longer in the group is helping the newcomer, and she is also helping herself as she reiterates what she has learned."

Donna Robbins was a member of a group eight years ago when she was being treated for breast cancer, and now she volunteers so the current members can see firsthand that there's light at the end of the tunnel. "I loved the group because I was able to talk about my feelings, my fears, my everything. I was able to cry, whatever, and I didn't feel stupid," says Robbins. "It's like I went through a bad dream, and now I'm comforting those women who are now going through that bad dream."

Marilyn Levine dropped in on a group after her seventh chemo. "I felt as if I'd been in the desert and was finally getting some water," says Levine. "I felt an immediate bonding to the other women. It was a feeling of safety and a place where I could go where other women understood, had to understand, all the multiple emotions I was feeling."

REASONS TO JOIN A SUPPORT GROUP

- **Reality check.** It proves you are not alone and provides a context for what you're experiencing.
- **Freebies.** It affords wig- and scarf-swapping opportunities.
- **Emotional outlet.** It is a place to talk (or laugh or cry) about things you can't discuss with other people.
- **Structure.** You can talk in a controlled environment; that is, with a trained leader who directs and moderates the conversation.
- **Community.** You develop friendships with women from all walks of life. Conversely, you can enjoy the company of women who are in the same boat while choosing not to continue these friendships past the time when you leave the group.
- **Education.** It's one-stop shopping for tips on coping and practical advice on how to handle doctors, family members, and children.
- **Mentoring.** It gives you an opportunity to pass along your wisdom to new women in the group, which also makes you feel good and encourages the healing process.
- **Safe house.** It may be the only place where you can vent frustration with how the rest of the world views

and treats you. Where else can you complain about the tone of voice of people who look at you probingly and ask, "How *are* you?"

❋ THE SPIEGEL STUDY

Joining a breast-cancer support group during treatment is one of the most important things you can do for yourself. So found the famous Spiegel study, published in the journal *Lancet* in 1989. It found that women who were members of support groups had a much healthier long-term outlook.

The survival rate after psychosocial intervention, which included those who joined support groups, "was on average more than double of those who did not."

The study had been designed to examine something else entirely—the use of acupuncture for the treatment of metastatic pain. The finding about the support groups was incidental, and may have been subject to bias because it was what is known as a "retrospective study." Nevertheless, there is no downside to group support.

HINT: DON'T NEGLECT YOUR GRAMMAR

One of Kleban's most difficult rows to hoe in group is making you see that you *had* the disease, past tense. By the time you've joined the group, you don't *have* it anymore.

"You need to understand that the treatment after surgery is just a preventive measure," says Kleban. "You have to learn to see yourselves as people who are not sick, who do not have an illness, but who are going through a protocol to prevent recurrence. Cancer often has a stigma in our society, but it's not a stigma or a death sentence, it's simply a diagnosis."

FIVE COMMON MISCONCEPTIONS ABOUT SUPPORT GROUPS

MYTH: It's depressing to hear other women's stories.
TRUTH: Actually, it's quite uplifting. Learning from other people's experiences comes from a long and valued tradition of intergenerational sharing through the ages, the handing down of wisdom. There is never a time when we cannot be helped and inspired by listening to others.

MYTH: It's hard to cry in front of strangers.
TRUTH: Honey, it's so *easy* to cry in front of strangers, you'll be amazed!

MYTH: Support groups aren't fun.
TRUTH: At times, you'll laugh so hard you won't know whether your runny eyes are a side effect of chemo or

mirth. Some sessions start out with a very serious tone and end up with rollicking fits of laughter, the liberating effect of having unburdened yourself of your worst fears.

MYTH: Your case is completely unique so a support group can't help you.
TRUTH: *You* are completely unique. Your case, on the other hand, is similar to thousands of others. There is comfort in numbers.

MYTH: You can't discuss your personal business with strangers.
TRUTH: You don't have to talk at all in the group if it makes you uncomfortable. A good group leader will not pressure you to contribute, because holding back may be part of what you need at that time. But you may find to your surprise that after a couple of sessions you enjoy participating. By the way, nothing is "too personal" among people who have looked into the abyss.

EXTRA HELP

Some hospitals and cancer organizations have outreach programs that can introduce you by phone or in person to someone who truly knows what you're going through. Memorial Sloan-Kettering Cancer Center, for example, has a magnificent program called Patient-to-Patient Volunteers, in which a database can match up a new patient with someone who had a similar diagnosis, right down to the same amount of lymph-node involvement. "This person acts as a role model for health and confidence," says Kleban. "She'll tell you from experience that after a couple of years, if you wake up with an unexplained pain, breast cancer will not be the first thing you're worried about. She can say yup, I was terribly depressed and upset too, and now I'm okay."

You can ask to talk to someone at any stage of your diagnosis and treatment. If you're considering breast reconstruction or are worried about the tattoo marks that guide the radiation treatments, you can find someone who will show you the real deal. Check the Resources section for organizations to call and clubs to join.

❋ GRANDMA GUSSIE

My mother's mother, Grandma Gussie—where did they get those names?—had a mastectomy when she was in her seventies. Although Grandpa Max was a prince of a fellow in other ways (he spoke many languages, told silly jokes, and did the laundry without complaint), he was not what you'd call an Alan Alda–type sensitive guy. I don't imagine Grandma and Grandpa ever sat down to discuss how they truly felt about this medical intrusion into their lives.

If there were any support systems available for women back then, Grandma certainly didn't seek them out. She was relatively secretive about her condition and went for chemo all by herself. This seems unthinkable. No hand to hold? No one to talk to? And those were the days when chemo was really rugged.

I don't know how Grandma felt about her breast cancer. She once showed me her "operation," which is how she referred both to her mastectomy scar and the general fact of having had cancer. But if she was looking for a wise and comforting child who could help her through this, she picked the wrong kid. I was totally freaked out. I had never really seen any adult naked, so the sight of an unreconstructed breast was rather alarming.

Grandma's cancer recurred, or so family anecdotes claim. She paid it no mind, as if it were a small inconvenience. She lived well into her eighties, entertained a profusion of gentleman callers after Grandpa died, and eventually succumbed to something else entirely.

But she was a person who probably would have loved a support group. One time when she had laryngitis, she went to choir practice anyway, "for the company."

A NOTE TO YOUR LOVED ONES

There are many ways in which one person's breast cancer is even harder on the people around her. Your life changes too, and you are expected to deal with it without complaint, yet you get little acknowledgment or training and no support groups so you can blow off steam. It's not easy being the caregiver half of a couple. And because women are so often the caregivers in their homes, it presents just as much a challenge to a spouse when roles are reversed.

After my diagnosis, I was galvanized to action, and had a lengthy schedule of doctor appointments and treatments. I had things to do. A cancer routine. Plus an endless supply of flowers and well-wishers. The people taking care of me—my mother, my sister, my friends— did not have such an easy time of it. One friend actually lost another friend over my illness, because she needed someone to talk to about her own fears for me, and the other friend was uncomfortable with that role.

Here's some advice for the people who have to deal with breast cancer from a position once removed:

- **Don't take it personally.** Women with breast cancer get cranky and fearful, even around such seemingly innocuous things as the six-month checkup (which is actually a big deal and causes some women to get sick in anticipation). If the patient lashes out at you, think first of the numerous breast cancer–related reasons that might have prompted it. Let it blow over.
- **Ask what you can do for her, and do it.** Don't be one

of those people who says, "Hey, if you need anything . . ." and then runs away. If she says she wants her own space, don't hover and ask if what she really wants is to talk it out. You can tell her that you're here to listen when and if she wants. And when that time comes, don't give advice unless she specifically asks for it. Men have a tendency to do that and it drives women crazy when all they want is a little support and understanding.

- **Don't share everything.** Sorry, but although honesty is usually the best policy, now is not the time to report all the obituaries you read in the paper. You don't have to walk on eggshells, but use discretion.

- **Find your own sounding board.** It's not easy being "the strong one," and you will need your own space in which to experience all those bottled-up fears and frustrations. Not everyone is up for that, as witnessed by my friend who lost a friend of her own. There are places like Gilda's Club that offer support groups for "friends and family of." My sister attended such a group during my illness and, although not usually a "joiner," found it very helpful.

- **No one-upmanship.** Or downmanship. Try not to get into martyr contests over who has suffered more, who needs more understanding, who is needier or more damaged. This leads nowhere and creates resentment.

8

❀

Body Language: Nutrition, Exercise, and Self-image

At some point in every breast-cancer patient's journey, she will likely wonder whether all this is because of something she ate. Something chocolate, perhaps. Or stale, or smoked, or caloric.

The simple answer is no, you did not bring your cancer on yourself. Nevertheless, it's an observable phenomenon: Breast-cancer patients find themselves naturally concerned with nutrition, because the disease and its treatments focus you on the particulars of your body every day. As you monitor side effects and changes in taste, you'll be keenly aware of what you eat and how your body reacts. Nothing motivates like a health scare, so you're likely to take renewed interest in avoiding the foods that rank high on the carcinogen menu: smoked meats, fried foods, chemical additives and preservatives, alcohol, and empty calories. If this sudden awareness galvanizes you to adopt healthier eating habits, so much the better.

Not everyone is willing or able to change a lifetime's eating habits at the drop of an ice-cream scoop. Nor should you feel compelled to do so at this time, as you have enough on your plate (so to speak). But if your habit is to eat poorly, you're not doing yourself any favors. Fatty diets and abdominal fat may increase your susceptibility to breast cancer (studies are still contradicting themselves on this one). Note that this is *not* the same as a direct causal link, such as the one that exists between cigarettes and lung cancer. It's possible, for example, that you could be rail-thin, an exemplar of portion control, grow your own vegetables, and still get breast cancer.

But if you're looking for a way to take control of your health and for a medical excuse to turn your life around, now is a propitious time.

Proper nutrition can help you cope with breast-cancer treatments as well as put you in good stead for the rest of your life. Optimally, you'd eat so admirably there'd be a shrine to you at the health food store, maybe your picture plus a sign saying "Notorious Soy Eater." But you needn't aim so high. Good nutrition during cancer can be as simple as eating specific foods that alleviate chemo side effects (such as crackers for nausea) or avoiding foods that, with your weakened ability to fight infection, are potential bacteria magnets (like sushi). The important thing is to continue getting enough nutrition to keep your strength up and help your body do its repair work between each chemo or radiation session.

I wasn't the only one casting a gimlet eye on my eating habits. My friend Meg referred to my kitchen as "the food museum," and one of the wonderful things she did for me during my treatments was to give it a complete overhaul. She went through the refrigerator and the cabinets, got rid of old and useless stuff, then replenished the shelves with healthy staples—the kind of food, she assured me, that is eaten by normal people, whoever *they* are.

The kitchen of my childhood was not a hospitable place, so where young ladies of another generation were rolling out pastry dough or putting up preserves for the winter, I was stuck on "defrost" and "reheat." My kitchen reflected this.

During Meg's kitchen blitz, I lay on the sofa while she rummaged through the shelves. There'd be an ominous silence, which meant she had stumbled across a food item that was unforgivable, and I'd hear her read off from a label some particularly heinous expiration date. "This can of peas remembers where it was when Kennedy was shot," muttered Meg darkly. Then there'd be a bustle of manic energy and the sounds of things being tossed in the garbage.

Occasionally Meg would come out from the kitchen with her hands on her hips and give me a look. "Jami Beth," she'd say, and I know there's trouble when she includes my middle name, "Jami Beth, why do you not own a kitchen sponge?"

There are very good reasons why I don't have a kitchen sponge, including "because," and "germs." But Meg didn't wait for the answer. These were rhetorical questions. There'd be the low rumble of Meg cursing under her breath and she'd emerge from the depths holding enough jars of capers to keep a Third World country in pasta puttanesca for decades. I have an unfortunate tendency to treat each shopping expedition as it if is the last time I will ever again have access to groceries. It is my nature to believe I've spent too much time in the bread lines during a harsh Russian winter.

Breast-cancer patients starting afresh on the nutrition front are often inspired by the famous study that equated traditional Japanese diets (low in animal protein and fat, high in vegetables) with lower incidences of breast cancer. What happened was that when women from Japan, a country typically low in breast-cancer rates, moved to Hawaii and adopted the high-fat American diet, their breast-cancer rate rose to match that of native-born Americans. But it is unclear which part of their new diet was the problem—the number of calories alone? The amount of fat? The type of fat? The levels of soy? Or fiber? The jury is still out.

In fact, the study of the Japanese women presents even more puzzles. A mammoth nutritional study conducted by Harvard's School of Public Health found that there was no statistically relevant correlation between eating fruits and vegetables in adulthood and avoiding breast cancer. The study, published in the *Journal of the American Medical Association* (JAMA) in February 2001, followed the fruit-and-vegetable habits of 351,825 women over the course of fifteen years.

Nevertheless, many women I know who had breast cancer began to eat lower and lower on the food chain until I just wanted to send a rare steak over to their table anonymously to restore their blood counts. I myself spent six months as a vegan, which takes vegetarianism to such extremes that you eat, like, nothing. "Waiter, I'll have the blue-plate special, but just the plate, nothing on it."

Actually, I enjoyed being a vegan and found it neither onerous nor depriving. It's just that, in the final tally, a life without cheese is too much to ask.

At least I now have a working kitchen with all the right things in the right places, thanks to Meg. If I can just find a friend who likes to houseclean, I'll be all set.

WEIGHT GAIN

I'm sorry to be the bearer of bad tidings, but, yes, there is a tendency for some breast-cancer patients to gain weight during chemo. The image of a cancer patient is of someone wasting away, but breast-cancer patients not only typically look in the pink, they also manage to put on a few pounds.

There are three major reasons for this. One is that you might get corticosteroids along with the chemo in your IV, and steroids make you eat like a Hoover. Steroids are what bodybuilders take (illegally) to help them bulk up. The first week or two on steroids, I staved off the cravings with boxes of dry breakfast cereal. I figured that the time and energy it took to gnaw through a box of Wheat Chex would more than offset the calories. After a while, I would follow up the crunchies with a steak.

Another inducement to gain weight is that when

chemo causes changes in taste, specific cravings may become intensified.

A third reason breast-cancer patients tend to gain weight is that . . . hello! We're *women!* We were *made* to gain weight. Our bodies are built to store up fat for childbearing, nursing, and the occasional famine. We have a smaller muscle mass than men, so it's harder for us to burn off the excess. And since each pound of fat is composed of 3,500 calories, we'd have to run an entire marathon to shed something that took a single Thanksgiving dinner to put on.

Add to this that women learn early in life to use food as compensation for anger, fear, anxiety, depression, and all those other emotions cancer brings out. Diagnosis: Breast cancer. Solution: The snack-food aisle of the grocery.

When I first heard about this weight-gain possibility, it was so depressing I had to eat a Twinkie. Before you freak out entirely, let me just emphasize that it's not the chemo itself that adds calories. It's what you eat during this time and whether you continue an exercise program that affects your weight.

Most women gain just a few pounds during treatment, and naturally there were several skinny minnies in my support group who didn't gain an ounce and didn't see what the big deal was. My sister's childhood friend Sharon Leventon* continued to swim almost every day and went through four complete cycles on her exercycle

---

*Although Sharon, like Laura mentioned earlier, was also a childhood friend of my sister's, Sharon did not give us a hamster like Laura did. This does not mean she is a lesser person.

odometer during her treatments, but that is partly because she also grapples with obsessive-compulsive disorder, which, as you can see, is not without its rewards.

NUTRITION

If emotional eating is a problem for you in everyday life, it will not magically go away with a cancer diagnosis. But here is the most wonderful sentence you may ever hear in your life: Now is *not* the time to go on a diet.

Please pause from your juice fast or 800-calorie-a-day miracle starvation plan to consider this: It is well documented that your body perceives a calorie-restricted diet as the precursor to total famine. Your body doesn't know you're just trying to look better in that cute little dress. It thinks another Ice Age is coming. Or that the bison are running thin this season. Not enough calories? Your body goes into red-alert mode and begins storing up fat for a rainy day. Even after you go back to eating normally, your body is cleverly thinking, "I'll just keep storing up a little *more* fat, because *you can't be too careful.*"

Thus begins the dreaded rebound effect, where you lose five pounds only to gain back ten. If there's any rebounding to do, you should do it on a trampoline and at least get some aerobic benefits.

Right now, during treatment, you can take a break from a lifetime of obsessing over your weight. You need your body operating at optimal speed, which it can't do if it thinks you are once again trying to starve it or trick it. You need to keep your strength up, because chemo and radiation sap you of energy, and food is the fuel that restores it. The emphasis now is on health, not numbers on a scale, and this is important for breast-cancer patients to remember because most women are likely to be going on or coming off some kind of diet plan that promised you the moon and gave you only midnight cravings.

At the same time, breast cancer does not give you license to binge. Your doctors don't want you to gain a lot of weight any more than they want you to lose it. The happy paradox is that the more you concentrate on nutrition, the easier it is to lose weight when the time comes, if you so desire. With your newfound education, you'll regard food in terms of what it offers your body's engine instead of what it compensates for from childhood.

When and if you get radiation, you will be forbidden(!) to lose weight, because in most cases a mold will be cast to your exact dimensions to help position you correctly for treatment. Having the mold cast is like sitting for a portrait—you have to stay still for a long stretch of time. You don't want to go through all that again, and you certainly don't want people saying about you, "She broke the mold!," in any way other than metaphorically.

I always brought a friend along to take notes for me at my doctor visits. During the first consultation with my oncologist, I asked just how strictly I'd have to watch what I ate during treatment. Meg was along for note-taking purposes, and what she wrote in the margins of her legal pad that day shows that she hadn't been a crack newspaper reporter all those years for nothing: "Ice cream? Why not!" It was underlined three times for emphasis.

An occasional dish of ice cream to sooth your inner child is fine. Acknowledge emotional eating for the temporary solace it is, and don't follow it up with self-punishing diet regimens.

> **Tip:** People who truly love you don't care about your weight, they care that you're alive. If you have a husband who's more concerned with how you look than with how you are feeling, take him directly to the 24-hour annulment drive-through. Or just threaten to.

SO, WHAT IS HEALTHY EATING?

I'll bet you already know the answer to this, but you keep hoping it will somehow change to "everything I want, all the time, plus a beer."

Sorry! It all comes back to what they've been telling you since you were a kid—*eat balanced meals in reasonable portions*. Those meals should include fruits, vegetables, whole grains, and legumes. If you're not vegetarian, it should include lean meat, fish, poultry, and dairy products. (By the way, if you don't currently eat five servings of fruits and vegetables each day as you should, build up to it slowly or your intestines will rebel.)

A "portion," by the way, is not everything that you can fit on a serving platter. For meat, it is a cut approximately the size of a deck of cards. For vegetables, it is usually half a cup. And one fruit equals a small apple, not the biggest melon in the patch.

The idea behind "balancing" the diet, or rotating through a combination of foods, is that you can't get all the vitamins and minerals you need from one source. Hence those lists of just what you can expect from kale versus what you get from cauliflower.

And what do you get from alcohol and rich desserts? Quite a lot, actually! You get tons and tons of calories! But you get very little else to nourish and sustain you. On top of those "empty" calories, you'll need even more calories that same day (or within a couple of days) from other food sources, the kind that have redeeming qualities like B vitamins or protein. So when my oncolgist said "Why not?" to a bowl of ice cream, he didn't mean I should live on the stuff. He meant that comfort food has its place in the arsenal.

You are not expected to memorize the lists of just which vitamins and minerals are in kale. It's enough to know that your diet should include "green leafy vegetables." By eating a balanced diet, you will get most of the vitamins your body requires.

Except possibly for vegetarians. They have a few special needs, because without animal protein they will eventually run low on vitamin B_{12}. And they need to seek out protein from such sources as soy and legumes so they don't carb themselves into oblivion. (If your idea of vegetarianism is nachos with cheese and breaded, deep-fried zucchini, then you might as well accept that you're not a vegetarian for health reasons.)

As for cooking healthy, again, most of you already know the drill. Steam or broil instead of frying. Choose whole grains over processed. Flavor with herbs and spices instead of oil, butter, and cheese. And try not to add fat, sugar, or salt during cooking.

Tip: A little salt on the top of your meal can fool your taste buds into thinking there's a lot of salt mixed all the way through it.

Tip: TV dinners have several compartments to them, but that does not mean they represent the major food groups.

HEALTHY EATING REQUIRES

• **Practice:** Changing a lifetime of bad habits doesn't happen overnight. One rule of thumb is that six weeks is required to make new habit "stick."

• **Patience:** Your zest for healthy eating may have come on suddenly. But this is not a race and you're not being graded on it. Set aside your anxiety about succeeding or failing and take the long view—healthy eating is for life.

• **Effort:** Eating right is not something that kicks in just during mealtimes. It's something you think about, read up on, and plan for. It may require heavy lifting—putting a pen to paper to note which groceries you need, menus you plan to follow, and foods you want to prepare in advance to freeze in small portions for instant meals throughout the week.

• **Knowledge:** You need a working knowledge of nutrients and how your body uses them in order to change your focus on food from something dangerous and seductive to something life-sustaining and practical. If, for example, the chemo has made your nails weak, you'll know you need protein, and you'll know which food sources offer it. Relax, this is not Ph.D. stuff.

• **Self-awareness:** Cultivate a connection with the signals from your body so that you can identify when you feel hunger, fullness, or cravings. It is not "wrong" to have an emotional craving for comfort food. But it's important to be able to distinguish that from physical hunger.

• **Self-love:** Think of the things you tell yourself when you "fall off the wagon." Would you ever turn that kind of anger on a child? A pet? Be as kind to yourself as you would be to a dear friend.

• **Choices:** Every mealtime is brimming with choices: broiled versus fried, for example, or lemon instead of butter. (Hint: Choose broiled; choose lemon. But you knew that.) Your meal is the culmination of a series of choices, including portion size.

• **Pleasure:** Just because eating is a basic need doesn't mean it can't be rewarding. Bring out the best in food by using fresh ingredients, adding spices, and savoring your meals. Food is not the enemy.

• **Motivation:** It's hard to stay focused on long-term goals like healthy eating, especially since the immediacy of breast cancer subsides. (Yes, it does!) You'll have to remind yourself on occasion why it's important to treat your body with tender, loving care.

Tip: Healthy eating is not a magic bullet. Plenty of healthy, athletic vegetarians get breast cancer too. Diet alone cannot prevent or cure breast cancer. So consider healthy eating a goal, and don't beat yourself up if you can't achieve that goal right now.

VITAMINS AND MINERALS IN A NUTSHELL

During breast-cancer treatments, your body may need more of some vitamins and minerals, less of others. Unless you are planning to go to sea for six months without any citrus fruits, you are unlikely to develop scurvy or other severe deficiencies. More likely, chemo may have you courting anemia. So, although you'll want to get your RDAs (recommended daily allowances) of vitamins and minerals, you don't need megadoses and shouldn't take any supplement without the advice of your doctor.

Vitamin A: A beta-carotene that improves vision. It is most commonly associated with carrots, making it easy to remember that orange foods such as apricots, yams, and cantaloupes have it. Here's another orangey food: tomatoes. If you were planning to improve your eyesight with a big bowl of pasta in tomato sauce, be aware that the tomato is highly acidic and should be avoided in all its forms if you have mouth sores or acid reflux.

Vitamin B$_1$ (thiamine): Among its many uses, thiamine helps prevent anemia, which is a possibility during chemo. Try eating whole-grain products, seafood, and beans. Brown rice, a good source of B$_1$, also helps chemo patients absorb excess stomach acid and acts against diarrhea (the BRAT diet: bananas, rice, apples, tea).

Vitamin B$_2$ (riboflavin): An excellent antioxident (something which helps round up the "free radicals" running around like hooligans in your body). Some women going into chemo are recently off diets, which deplete the body of this vitamin. If a nutritionist finds this to be the case, increase your consumption of milk, cheese, yogurt, green leafy vegetables, fruits, bread, cereals, and organ meats.

Vitamin B$_3$ (niacin): Useful in protecting against cardiovascular disease. Found in lean meats, fish, and poultry. Breast-cancer patients who are vegetarians need to supplement their supply of this vitamin.

Vitamin B$_6$: A very good worker bee when it comes to cell maintenance, particularly red blood cells, whose production is hampered by chemo. It is found in meats, whole grains, and brewer's yeast.

Vitamin B$_{12}$: Associated with higher energy levels and useful in combating anemia, this is a water soluble vitamin that leaves the system overnight, needing replenishment more than quantity. You'll get all you need of it from fish, dairy products, organ meats, eggs, beef, and pork, which means vegetarians have to be diligent.

Vitamin C: Helps wounds heal (important for platelet and white-cell reduction during chemo) and reduces the suffering associated with the common cold, among other things. It will not cure cancer, although there are those who would like to believe it does. Save your money and eat citrus fruits (like oranges and grapefruit) and fresh vegetables. Other good sources: strawberries and potatoes.

Vitamin D: This is actually a term for several hormones that are activated by the ultraviolet radiation of sunlight. It is vital for bone mineralization. You can find a small amount in some densely rich food sources, like liver, egg yolks, fatty fish, and milk fat. Or you can take a quick walk outdoors (fifteen to twenty minutes) and get your vitamin D that way. During radiation treatments, avoid the sun entirely near your chest, arm, and back, and always use a sunscreen when outdoors.

Vitamin E: An antioxident that relaxes muscle cramps. Many people break open capsules to apply to healing scar tissue, although your genetic predisposition has more of a say in how your scars heal than anything you rub on them. Before you apply anything topically, check with your doctor, especially during radiation treatments. You can get this vitamin from eggs, vegetables, whole-grain cereal, nuts, and seeds. Also enriched flour, leafy greens, and vegetable oil.

Vitamin K: Helps blood clot, and during chemo you'll need all the help you can get in that department. You can get enough of it from vegetables and dairy products. It is also produced by certain bacteria, so yogurt makes a healthy breeding ground for it in the stomach.

Minerals: A couple of these inorganic substances bear mentioning. Calcium is particularly important to women because chemo can temporarily halt your period and thus reduce the estrogen flow that protects against bone loss. You will be happy to know that ice cream contains calcium. And so do other milk and dairy products, as well as salmon, green leafy vegetables, and tofu. Iron levels are also important to chemo patients, because they fall along with the decrease in red blood cells. A pronounced deficiency may cause delays in your treatment, and will undoubtedly contribute to fatigue. Red and organ meats are high in iron. Other sources include poultry and fish. I ate a lot of roast beef at my birthday party and at my next chemo session the nurse looked up from my red cell counts in awe. Vegetarians need to be diligent about getting enough iron. An iron supplement sounds simple, but note that it can cause constipation, diarrhea, and other intestinal discomforts, a bad combination with chemo side effects of the digestive tract.

SPECIAL NUTRITIONAL NEEDS
DURING CHEMO

- **Choose wisely.** Don't eat your favorite foods before a chemo session, just in case you develop an unpleasant association between the two.
- **Avoid alcohol.** Here you've been trying to flush as much water through your system as possible, and you're considering a glass of pure dehydration? Also, if you have mouth sores, don't even think about it.
- **Don't overeat.** Last night's celebratory meal can be tonight's queasy regret.
- **Watch out for germs.** Because you are more susceptible to infection during chemo, carefully wash all foods like vegetables and fruits before eating, and avoid foods that you just know are trouble (like sushi, carpaccio, and anything raw). In the same vein, use bottled instead of tap water.

PREVENTING NAUSEA WITH NUTRITION

In addition to taking antiemetic drugs after chemo, you can manage nausea with some simple nutritional methods.

Eating right to prevent nausea is not so awful. You won't be limited to hospital-like Jell-O cubes, so quit yer whining. Remember that chemo is administered in cycles, and the body recovers between each cycle, so we're talking about only a few days of nausea every few weeks.

Queasiness can be quelled by eating frequent light

meals that don't fill up your stomach, eating foods that are bland and not at extremes of temperature or spice, and keeping dry crackers, popcorn, or cereal around for snacks that soak up stomach acid. Stay away from high-fat foods.

You should be drinking a lot (although not necessarily at mealtimes) to combat problems with the kidney and bladder that can develop while taking cyclophosphamide, which can irritate the bladder, causing bleeding and, in very rare cases, bladder cancer years later. Increased fluid intake increases the flow through the kidneys and bladder, thereby decreasing the concentration of the drug and reducing the risk. Clear cool liquids are welcome, and sucking on a frozen apple-juice ice cube is fun. (You can freeze a trayful with popsicle sticks to make them easier to handle. Children have all the right ideas.)

It's not totally necessary, but you might try letting sodas go flat before drinking them. It's less irritating to the stomach. Ginger root and peppermint are tummy soothers and can be found in herbal teas. But note that many popular beverages with the word "ginger" in the title contain only natural (or unnatural) ginger flavoring, and not the actual root itself.

You may experience changes in taste during chemo. What was once your favorite food now looks like a day-old witch's brew. Slight odors of staleness or mustiness may trigger the gag reflex. Eat only what appeals to you, and don't feel guilty about turning down the offerings of kindly friends and neighbors.

Try to keep fresh air circulating through the house—

leave windows open, use fans if necessary. Even if it's a polar winter, try to air out the house occasionally.

You can distract yourself from nausea by splashing cold water on your face, doing breathing and relaxation exercises, and listening to music.

This probably goes without saying, but you need to aid your digestive process as much as possible, so don't lie on your back after a full meal! And don't wear tight clothing. Pantyhose should be outlawed anyway, I believe, and you certainly don't want to be wearing anything that requires you to lie on your back in order to zip it up—not when your stomach is making threatening noises of doom.

Eat foods that are minimally processed to avoid the extra fat and salt. Red meat is hard to digest, although remember my success with the roast beef and the blood counts.

PHYTOESTROGENS

You hear this word bandied about in discussions of breast cancer. Phytoestrogens (or isoflavones) are plant estrogens, found in plentiful supply in soy. They are weaker than the estrogens you get from animal protein, an excess of which has been associated with breast cancer. When the aforementioned Japanese women who moved to Hawaii were studied for their changes in diet, soy came to light as an excellent substitute for animal protein. You can get it from tofu, soy milk, roasted soy nuts, and soy protein powder. Many coffee chains offer soy on request, even if you don't see it on the menu.

EXERCISE

For a year and a half before I was diagnosed with breast cancer, I was working out daily in my home gym, one of those mail-order setups. I also had a personal trainer, Norman, who was a neighbor and thus knew whether I was faking it if I tried to cancel because I was "sick" or "out of town." He had only to walk across the hall to see if I was malingering.

I loved weight training with Norman. I flexed my biceps for everyone and they could barely hide their delight. (Well, I like to *think* it was delight.) It gave me great pleasure to feel fit and energetic. "Strong like bull," I'd announce in a fake Russian accent, rolling up my sleeve and flexing yet again.

After my diagnosis, I experienced a lot of conflict about exercising. It seemed unfair that I had finally adopted a healthy lifestyle only to find out I had cancer. (The tumor undoubtedly predated my addiction to working out, so they were unrelated events.) Exercise had become so important to me that I worried about how breast cancer would interfere with it. For people who have had lymph nodes removed during axillary dissection, heavy lifting (more than fifteen pounds) is not recommended because of the risk of incurring **lymphedema.** And the creepy-crawly arm and hand exercises all breast cancer patients practice after surgery seemed puny and insufficient substitutes for the sweaty, grunting workouts I enjoyed B.C. (Before Cancer).

I obsessed over whether I would ever be able to go back to weight training. I thought it tragically unfair that cancer had nipped my new hobby in the bud. And yet I did not resume a sensible exercise program until well after my treatment. I rationalized that I had to conserve energy for the big battle ahead, and I felt uncertain about my changing physical limitations.

There was no reason why I couldn't have continued exercising, at least in a scaled-down way, during treatment. I was still strong like bull from the weight training I'd done up until my surgery, and that strength is undoubtedly a large part of why my cancer treatments were not all that onerous. Exercise is one of the great natural coping tools. It helps regulate body functions and mood, revs up the metabolism, brings oxygen to the brain, and just makes you feel jazzed all over.

"Exercise helped me tremendously," says my friend's mother, Teresa. "I walked. Even during treatments, I dragged myself out for short periods. The worst I could do was to lie in bed trying to rest. That was detrimental to my mind, which then affected my whole body. I felt sick if I stayed in bed. Even when I was very tired, I focused my energy and tried to walk. As soon as I finished chemo and all the way through radiation, I went to the gym, did the bicycle and weights. I started with one-pound weights on the surgery side, and worked up to three pounds, five, eight, and twelve. Now I do fifteen on that arm. I also started aerobics, which gave me a lot of energy. Of course you have to modify how much you do because your energy is not the same. But I found that the more I did, the more I could do."

I'm not suggesting you do power lifting or complete

an Iron Man competition during treatment. In fact, I'd have to advise against that. You should check with your doctor about what you can and cannot attempt, and you must use true common sense to decipher when you are too tired, thirsty, or emotionally depleted to continue. *Always* be careful about hurting or overtaxing the arm on the side where you had surgery.

If you feel too weak to do any exercise, then by all means, don't! But at least try to take a few walks every week like Teresa did. It's a guaranteed mood lifter and will generate even more energy down the road. It only takes about twelve minutes of brisk walking to start feeling those wonderful endorphins fan out through your body, so if you're feeling sluggish or depressed, you can always tell yourself, Start moving! Happiness is just twelve minutes away!

Gentle Exercise Tips

- **More reps, less weight.** If you've been exercising regularly, continue to do so but scale back your normal routine to accommodate lower energy levels. For example, do more reps (repetitions) at lower weights rather that increasing the load when working with machines or dumbbells.
- **Simple movement.** If you have not been exercising, you don't want to start a big-time regimen just now. However, some mild aerobic activity—like taking a walk—is important and will bring more oxygen to your system. Try taking a twenty-minute walk a few

times a week with a friend. Wear comfortable shoes and loose clothing and carry water in a backpack so your arms can swing freely.

- **Move that arm.** Continue the hand and arm exercises they teach you in the hospital after surgery to prevent "frozen shoulder." This includes gentle stretching with your fingers doing a spidery climb up a wall, opening and closing your fist, doing wrist and elbow bends, and lifting your arms over your head. Every movement should be slow and methodical.

- **Avoid germs.** If you belong to a gym, avoid the steam and sauna rooms where germs are having a frat party. In the same vein, wear flip-flops in the communal showers.

- **Swim aerobics.** Swimming or just "running laps" in the pool is a wonderful, gentle exercise, but not during radiation when your skin is sensitive to the chlorine.

- **Elevate your heart rate.** If you are an old hand at exercise and know your limitations, give yourself the occasional endorphin rush by jumping on the stationary bike or treadmill for twenty minutes whenever you're feeling anxious or depressed. Remember to stay hydrated. If you feel dehydrated or headachy, you need a lot more liquid to replenish yourself than you'd suspect, so keep drinking even if you don't feel thirsty.

- **Keep it simple.** Heavy weight lifting, contact sports, and activities where you might fall are ill-advised during chemo because of the body's difficulties with bruising and blood clotting.

> **Tip:** Here is the official list of exercises to avoid during adjuvant treatment: Wilderness survival, helicopter skiing, World Wrestling Federation smackdowns, white-water rafting on the Amazon.

EVERGREEN EXERCISES

- Beginner's yoga
- Brisk morning walk
- Pedaling on a stationary bike just hard enough to break a mild sweat
- Low-impact aerobics, either at a gym class or with an exercise video

LYMPHEDEMA

Those who have had removal of lymph nodes under their arms (axillary dissection) must take certain precautions to avoid getting lymphedema, a painful swelling of the arm for which there is currently no cure. Because the lymph drainage system has been compromised by the surgery, too much lymphatic fluid pumping into that arm will collect in the spaces between tissue cells and have trouble draining back out. Factors that draw lymph into the arm include injury and infection.

No doubt the hospital has already shown you postsurgical arm exercises or given you a booklet describing them. Throughout your life, you'll want to be vigilant about protecting the arm on the side where you had surgery. Vigilance doesn't mean living the rest of your life in fear. It means a heightened awareness, so that if you do get a cut or insect bite, you treat it quickly and don't let any swelling go unnoticed. Here are some things to watch for:

- Prevent and/or monitor insect bites, cuts, scrapes, and bruises.
- Pay attention to a "tight" feeling or noticeable swelling on that side.
- Do not put a blood-pressure cuff on the arm that has had axillary dissection.
- Do not have injections or blood drawn on that side.
- Carry a travel-size tube of antibacterial ointment, especially if you are doing something outdoorsy where you can get scratched.
- Do not carry heavy shoulder or shopping bags on that side. Change arms every now and then if you're carrying a handbag.
- Light exercise on that side is good for you. Strong muscles help pump the fluid back into circulation. But check with your doctor before undertaking any new exercise regimen and get a clear reading on how much weight you should attempt to lift, if any.
- Don't wear tight jewelry or watchbands on that side. If you always wear the same thing on that arm and it's feeling tighter lately, see your doctor.
- Keep the area away from the sun's rays or use a lotion with SPF15 or higher. Preferably higher.

- If you use a compression sleeve, make sure to wear it on airplanes.

SELF-IMAGE

There isn't a woman in America who doesn't think there's something wrong with at least one part of her body. Breast cancer provides an additional source of worry about body image.

Weight is only one part of the equation. Research on overweight suggests that bodies are genetically programmed to achieve a certain weight range. At the low end of that weight range, your metabolism slows down, making it easy to gain a few pounds so that the body will return to what it thinks is the status quo. At the high end of that weight range, it speeds up to burn more calories. If you've been keeping a photo of a waif supermodel on your refrigerator as inspiration, take it down right now— she achieved that stick frame through the miracle of genetics and the kind of pharmaceutical help that only a supermodel can afford.

Women also worry about their surgery scars, and whether that will hinder sex. Are you in a relationship with the typical guy? Then I have news for you—it won't hinder sex. Anyway, studies have shown that women are far more critical of themselves than the men they're worried about disappointing.

I may be perverse, but after the initial shock, I came to love my lumpectomy scar. Once I got used to it, it became only an afterthought in the bedroom. I was single when I was being treated for cancer, and although I didn't feel particularly sexy during treatment, I continued to date. In fact, since the kind of guy looking for a centerfold wasn't interested in me even before surgery, it seemed I attracted a better class of men, none of whom seemed the least bothered by the scar.

However, I am already a veteran of several surgeries, and although I quickly adjusted to my lumpectomy scar, I was not always so sanguine. Major surgery brings out a multitude of unforeseen feelings about the body being violated and its geography altered. And losing a breast to a mastectomy, whether or not it is followed by reconstruction, is an emotionally devastating situation that is not easily overcome. It may take all your resources—time, patience, friends, and very slow going with your loved one— before you feel comfortable enough with your body again.

Meg,* a comic who had reconstruction after her mastectomy, "had boyfriends throughout" treatment, some of whom found her cancer "too intense," and has now settled down with a keeper. She recalls asking one how he felt about scars, to which he replied, "I think they're sexy." To which *she* replied, "Have I got a treat for you!"

The women in my support group often discussed whether it was harder to be married or single. There is no right answer to this. Accepting your new body is a product of many factors, including your own personality and who you have in your corner. Having a loving, patient partner is optimal, but no one's a saint and your partner

---

*This is not the same Meg as the Meg who reorganized my kitchen earlier in this chapter. It is just a sudden, inexplicable surfeit of Megs.

can snap over something minor just as easily as over something major. Sex may be tough going for both of you at first. Try to be clear about what you need and what your fears are, and allow your partner to express the same.

Anyway, intimacy is about so much more than sex. If you can maintain or reestablish intimacy—cuddling, sharing, touching, and looking into each other's eyes—more can follow in due course.

For single women, there can be anxiety over how and when to tell (or show) a new partner what's happened to you. How your new guy reacts will certainly be a test of his character, and also a test of a fledgling relationship. One woman I spoke to got a divorce during her treatments, and it was not until four years later that she even felt like making an effort at dating again, although she was quite cheerful about the wait. ("Wasn't ready!" she crowed.) Several women with lumpectomies said their scars were virtually invisible and made no difference in their love lives. The single women I know kvetch about men the way all single women do, with or without breast cancer.

Plenty of women were more concerned about being bald, or about how their hair grew in when it was still downy or stubbly, than they were with their breasts. For years after treatment, many women still discuss, with anxiety, the particulars of how their hair came back (straighter or curlier or grayer). Again, it is probably a displacement of a general fear of cancer and mortality, and that's something that may never entirely go away.

The key, as always, is to love yourself as you are, and to accept others as they are as well. I know, easier said than done. But this is the task that confronts everyone, not just breast-cancer patients. You must always keep in mind that you are more than just your body and that cancer doesn't define you, even if it unduly occupies your thoughts for a long time.

LOOK GOOD, FEEL BETTER

The day after my lumpectomy, I was in a mood. Something Linda Blair-ish, circa *The Exorcist*. And yet, this must have been carnival day at the hospital, because every few minutes there'd be another cheery nurse hauling me out of bed for something or other.

I was just working up to a good feel-sorry-for-myself cryfest, or maybe an hour-long journey to the toilet and back (involving such activities as "sitting up" and "moving around"), when once again the nurses intervened in my plans. "It's time for the Look Good, Feel Better class!" they chirped.

I tried to swat them away. "I look terrible! I feel lousy!" I protested.

"Well, that's just the point!" they argued, pulling the bedclothes from my clenched fists and fetching my koala-bear fuzzy slippers. I joined about a dozen equally glum breast-cancer patients pushing their IVs ahead of them who were not inclined just then to look on the bright side.

Later that day, I entertained my first wave of visitors. They were amazed to find me sitting up, making jokes, and glowing with that glow you get after a professional (free!) makeup lesson.

"You look good!" they said, sounding a bit surprised.

And I felt even better.

The Look Good, Feel Better program is a community-based, free national service. It was begun in 1990 by the Cosmetic, Toiletry and Fragrance Association Foundation in cooperation with the American Cancer Society and the National Cosmetology Association.

The class is held in hospitals, cancer and community centers, and sometimes even after hours in beauty salons. It is led by one or two beauty professionals who have donated their time to educate breast-cancer patients on how to apply cosmetics. (In rural areas, they'll mail you a videotape for a home session.) It's not only a boost to a woman's natural sense of self-confidence, it also serves a very practical function—teaching women how to mask treatment side effects ranging from changes in skin tone to hair loss.

Among the tips they give is how to draw a convincing eyebrow, first by having you concentrate on the brow you still, at least temporarily, possess. Where does it begin, curve, and end? What sort of brush will give it a natural feathered look?

They also advise on how to choose a wig, wrap a turban, and tie a bandanna.

A free makeup lesson is always welcome, beauty tips even more so. But here's the glory of the Look Good, Feel Better program—they give you a whopping big bag of free, brand-name makeup, all of which has been donated to the cause. Cancer patients are not so freaked out that they can't appreciate a quality goody bag. I mean, this was at least a hundred dollars' worth of top-shelf items—lipsticks, blush, moisturizer, cleanser. Everyone who signs up gets a different assortment; mine included some alabaster glitter for those nights when I might want to go straight from chemo to the disco.

The nationwide program depends not only on the companies that donate makeup, but on professionals who volunteer their time to show participants how to apply it. Part of the session is a typical makeup class, beginning with the essentials of skin care and moving on to how to blend colors and, if you're not a model, how to locate your cheekbones. I tried to feign boredom and above-it-all-ness, but actually I learned a thing or two, including that powder should always be applied in downward strokes so as not to catch the light the wrong way, whereas foundation is applied in circular motions to blend in as much as possible.

Gently and unobtrusively, the class also addresses such issues as how to compensate for the possible loss of eyebrows and eyelashes, or for the haggard look that accompanies nausea and fatigue. At the time, I dismissed some of this advice as definitely not applying to me. Can you say "denial"?

Later, when my eyebrows and eyelashes did indeed fall out and made me look like a one-person alien invasion, the makeup tips I had back-burnered came in handy.

MANICURES AND PEDICURES

I know this will just devastate some women, but buck up and be strong: throughout chemo treatments you may have to stop having manicures and pedicures.

If you refuse to stop—I mean, if you're a beauty-treatment junkie who can't give up her weekly nail salon fix without the aid of rehab—then there are precautions you can and should take.

Bring your own instruments. Even if your local salon looks clean and seems to sterilize everything, don't count on it. During those times when your blood counts are low, you don't want your tender, immunity-challenged skin coming into contact with bacteria from—ugh!—someone else's gnarly old feet.

Don't cut the cuticles. Your low platelet count means poor blood clotting abilities and easy bruising, and your low white-cell count means poor infection-fighting. Push the cuticle back, if necessary, but don't cut it.

Here's news you may as well absorb now: Paula Begoun, who is like the Ralph Nader of the skin-care industry, points out in her book *The Beauty Bible* that you should *never* cut your cuticles! "The best way to keep your nails healthy, whole and as free from problems as possible is to keep your cuticles intact," she writes. "The cuticle is the body's form of protection for the area between the exposed, dead part of the nail and the living matrix the nail grows from. Anything that tampers with this seal puts the nail at risk."

Tell the pedicurist to lighten up. You know those lovely lower-leg massages the pedicurist usually throws in while your feet are soaking? Your low platelet count means you are easily bruised. The women at my local salon usually follow up the massage with one of those jackhammer-punch techniques that is a little on the bone-jarring side to begin with. I'd skip that part, or at least tell them to go easy.

Skip the salon. Just for this time in your life, ask a loved one to paint your toenails and tenderly massage your feet. Very sexy stuff, you know. Remember the scene in *Bull Durham* where Kevin Costner painted Susan Sarandon's toenails? If your loved one does a good enough job, you might want to pretend the ban on professional pedicures is a lifelong thing. While you're at it, you can also pretend there was a study that found it is medically imperative that partners remember your birthday and take out the garbage.

CHEERFUL IS AS CHEERFUL DOES

The biggest obstacle to coming to terms with breast cancer, according to support-group maven Roz Kleban, is "how to defend yourself against the proliferation in pop literature of the idea that you can control the future of your illness with positive thinking, that you created your cancer. Patients are victimized by that theory and believe it, and are left in a situation where they are torturing themselves with recrimination and fear. This is a terrible disservice. It's a theory promulgated by people who never had a major illness, that if you're cheerful and positive, you'll be okay. It's an oxymoron to tell someone they have cancer and then tell them to be positive and optimistic."

Also, says Kleban, it's unfair that the only population asked to be positive at all times are cancer patients, "while the rest of us can mope around."

Kleban sees women suffering all the time from the tyranny of the positive-thinking Nazis. "Sometimes they feel it is their job to search quietly for whatever their deficiency is. They're ashamed. It's difficult enough to deal with breast cancer, and to add shame and guilt on top of it makes it that much more difficult. If you start out with not the greatest sense of self-esteem, and then you get breast cancer, such a viewpoint is perfect to reinforce your bad feelings about yourself," says Kleban. "There are plenty of women who are intelligent and accomplished yet who harbor a sense of being inadequate. They keep this inadequacy private, like a secret, but they see cancer as a confirmation, that now the news is out."

Tip: A Netherlands study of 9,705 women confirmed that there was no such thing as a "cancer personality." While depression, anger, and stress may contribute to the development of coronary disease, these emotions have never been shown to have any connection with breast cancer.

FOUR SELF-CARE SUGGESTIONS

- When you treat yourself to self-care products, skip your normal consumer instincts and spring for the stuff in the gorgeous packaging. You'll feel great using it every day.
- Unless you're Morticia Addams, don't dress all in black. Sure, it matches your mood. But the more you try to hide behind dark colors and make yourself invisible, the more morose you'll feel. (On the other hand, avoid orange spandex with sequins if you possibly can.)
- Get a free makeover at a nearby department store. They offer them all the time. Because of possible hair loss and changes in skin tone during chemo, your regular colors might not be working.
- If you're self-conscious about your hair, change the focus of attention by wearing interesting earrings or other jewelry.

❀

9

Alternative Versus Complementary Therapies

Meg, a professional comic who does not suffer fools gladly, reports that a friend urged her not to do chemo. "Don't you know what chemo does to your body?" said the friend. "Evidently," says Meg, "she didn't know what *cancer* does to the body."

I too had a well-meaning friend who tried to discourage me from obtaining medical treatment. There are people out there who think of mainstream medicine as sinister. They may try to steer you to "alternatives," which are unproven theories that haven't been properly tested (if at all), and which operate in secrecy outside the parameters of legitimate medicine.

There has been an undeniable surge of interest in what is called "alternative and complementary medicine." But although they are usually pronounced in the same breath, the two are very different things, almost strangers to each other. Complementary therapies, when used in addition to medical care, are harmless and possibly helpful. (Keeping a journal isn't likely to cause you any lasting damage unless you start writing some really bad poetry.) On the other hand, "alternative medicine" is unproven, unregulated, often expensive, and far from risk-free despite claims of containing all-natural ingredients. (Arsenic is nature's own, by the way, but that doesn't make it safe to drink.)

The purveyors of quack alternatives coopt the language of science and the imagery of nature to push their wares. "The more destructive a product is to either the environment or our own bodies, the more prominently images of nature figure in the way it is advertised, as can be seen in ubiquitous billboards and subway posters for cigarettes, alcohol, and cars, all of which feature picturesque waterfalls and mist-enshrouded groves of giant sequoias. Advertisers use nature much as they use children, as the detergent for morally problematic commodities," writes the culture critic Daniel Harris.

Nowhere are images of health and nature called upon more often than in the alternative-medicine racket. Products are described as natural and benign, and they are marketed to imply that taking them will connect you in some cosmic way to ancient, presumably nobler, cultures.

"While people are trying these supposedly more natural remedies, their cancer is growing, and by the time they come in for care, it's much beyond where it should have been," cautions Dr. Barrie Cassileth, Ph.D., head of

Memorial Sloan-Kettering Cancer Center's ground-breaking Integrative Medicine Service, which offers safe and soothing complementary therapies to cancer patients.

Dr. Cassileth conducted a survey, published in the *Journal of Medicine*, that found that 8 to 10 percent of newly diagnosed patients "go directly to alternative therapists for some length of time." This is dangerous stuff, because it delays treatment, allowing the cancer cells time to multiply exponentially. Dr. Cassileth offers a good rule of thumb for discriminating between alternative and complementary therapies: "I define alternative therapies according to the way they are promoted. If it is promoted as a cancer cure, or a viable treatment, or a reasonable and true option, that's an alternative therapy," and thus, something to be avoided.

Another clue is to follow the money. If a Web site promotes an unproven treatment and sells it too, keep surfing! Dr. Cassileth advises avoiding all commercial Web sites because of the vested interest in their products. Instead, turn to Web sites run by The American Medical Association (AMA), or the American Cancer Society (ACS), which has a separate section on alternative therapies.

"Quacks tend to be isolated from established scientific facilities and associations. They report their results through nonmedical channels rather than scientific journals," according to *The Health Robbers: A Close Look at Quackery in America*. "Sometimes their cure is 'secret' or bears their own name. They claim persecution by the medical profession or government agencies. Typically, they keep scanty records or no records at all. Many demand large amounts of cash in advance for methods that cost very little to administer."

IT DOESN'T CURE CANCER IF

- There's no proof except testimonials.
- You need a passport to find the only clinic that dispenses it.
- All the ingredients are too secret to reveal.
- Its inventor is currently under federal investigation.
- There are no records of former patients.
- Its puveyors claim the government doesn't want you to know about it.
- In addition to curing cancer, it purportedly accomplishes a series of ill-defined tasks such as "restoring harmony."

Science and law both demand that anyone who makes a health claim bear the burden of proof. The American Cancer Society's Committee on Questionable Methods of Cancer Management has three questions that must be answered:

- Has the method been objectively demonstrated in the peer-reviewed scientific literature to be effective?
- Has the method shown potential for benefit that clearly exceeds the potential for harm?

- Have objective studies been correctly conducted under appropriate peer review to answer these questions?

✳ IS LAUGHTER THE BEST MEDICINE?

Alternative treatments that cannot prove their effectiveness often resort to testimonials, which sound reassuring but which are medically useless. "Without corroborative evidence from other sources, or physical proof of some sort, ten anecdotes are no better than one, and a hundred anecdotes are no better than ten," says Michael Shermer, author of *Why People Believe Weird Things.*

Shermer gives an example. Let's say you know someone who credits Marx Brothers movies with curing her cancer. Before you hold a press conference, you'd have to set up a controlled experiment with properly diagnosed and matched cancer patients, in which some of them watch Marx Brothers movies, some watch Hitchcock, some watch the news, and some watch nothing. "Then we need to deduct the average rate of remission for this type of cancer and then analyze the data for statistically significant differences between the groups," writes Shermer.

Of course, if watching Marx brothers movies makes you laugh, and that feels good, by all means pop *Duck Soup* into the VCR.

QUACKPOT THEORIES

William Lane, Ph.D., who wrote the 1992 book *Sharks Don't Get Cancer* and its follow-up *Sharks Still Don't Get Cancer*, and his son, Andrew J. Lane, were fined one million dollars in April 2000 by the Federal Trade Commission for "falsely representing that clinical studies have shown that [shark cartilage] is effective in preventing, treating, and curing cancer."

The theory behind taking powdered-shark food supplements is that it will inhibit the growth of blood vessels that feed cancer cells, a process called antiangiogenesis. The rationale is that cartilage has relatively few blood vessels, and sharks have a lot of cartilage.

But just because you can see the effects of antiangiogenesis in a lab does not mean that if you swallow a piece of shark your body will respond like that test tube. As Larry Norton of Memorial Sloan-Kettering Cancer Center is fond of pointing out, chickens don't get breast cancer, but eating poultry won't guarantee the same for humans.

Further studies showed that shark cartilage was totally inactive in those patients who took it. Most tellingly, it turns out that sharks *do* get cancer, including chondromas—cancer of the cartilage.

The Registry of Tumors in Lower Animals at George Washington University has documented dozens of tumors in sharks, including chondromas. Dr. John C. Harshbarger, the registry's director, says: "It appears that sharks are being destroyed needlessly to exploit desperate people based on erroneous information."

❋ HOMEOPATHY

The good news about homeopathy is that it probably can't hurt you, because if made according to strict instructions, it doesn't contain even one molecule of the original medicine that was supposed to be in it.

In the late 1700s, Samuel Hahnemann, a German physician, came up with the idea that like cures like, or, the law of similars. If you have a hangover and you drink "some hair of the dog what bit you," you are doing something along the same lines.

Studies that appeared to support homeopathy were Swiss-cheesed with design flaws, as reported in the *Review of Epidemiology*. That aside, consider that Hahnemann prescribed multiple dilutions of his medicines until they passed what is called Avogadro's number (6.023 times 10 to the 23rd power), beyond which there are no molecules of the original substance left. The water in which the substance was dissolved is supposed to "remember" what floated in it, a disturbing thought if you consider the other things that might have also floated in it.

And yet homeopathic elixirs are not without risks. As *Consumer Reports* notes, "Ineffective drugs are dangerous drugs when used to treat serious or life-threatening disease. Moreover, even though homeopathic drugs are essentially nontoxic, self-medication can still be hazardous. Using them for a serious illness or undiagnosed pain instead of obtaining proper medical attention could prove harmful or even fatal."

DANGER ZONE

Here are some of the most controversial "cures":

Topical treatments. Since ancient times, folk wisdom has prescribed various ointments and preparations, most of them of a dubious nature and some of them quite revolting, to spread on the breasts in the event of disease. Even today there are those who claim that slathering noxious concoctions on the chest will magically ward off cancer. Your radiation oncologist may suggest a cream in case the skin is inflamed, but that's about as far as it goes.

Special diets. It's fine to go vegetarian or eat soy, as long as you get enough nutrition. But you have to realize that there is *nothing* edible at this time that has been proven to cure or reliably prevent cancer. Nevertheless, there are programs that offer cancer patients such regimens as coffee enemas or diets with specific balances of minerals. Never substitute such a plan for medical treatment, and always confer with your oncologist before making a drastic change in diet during treatment.

Herbal tea. Don't look to the tea leaves alone for a clean bill of health. Herbal teas have been around a long time, and are rich in antioxidants called polyphenals. But the specific notion that tea can cure cancer got a boost in the 1930s when an Ontario nurse named René Caisse started brewing batches of Essiac for the neighborhood. Caisse claimed to have gotten the "miracle" recipe from Native Americans (although she grandly named the product after herself; Essiac is Caisse spelled backward). It is a mixture of four herbs: Indian (or turkey) rhubarb, sheepshead sorrel, slippery elm, and burdock root. Studies of Essiac have not shown anti-tumor activity in animals or patients, which does not mean you can't serve it alongside a scone. The problem, according to someone who tried it, is that it tastes terrible.

Going braless. One theory that surfaced was that tight clothing constricts the lymphatic system, and that women who wear their bras twenty-four hours a day are 125 times more likely to get breast cancer. I wonder who these women are who wear their bras twenty-four hours a day. In any case, doing away with bras sounds like the kind of medical advice a frat party would give.

Apricot pits. The actor Steve McQueen helped put laetrile on the map when he visited a clinic in Mexico, only to die of cancer anyway. This substance found in peach and apricot pits "heads the all-time list of quack cancer remedies," opines Stephen Barrett, M.D., who has conducted extensive research into purported cancer treatments. A clinical trial at the Mayo Clinic failed to prove any tumor-reducing benefit to cancer patients from laetrile. Several of the patients experienced cyanide toxicity; laetrile contains the chemical amygdalin, which can break down into a toxic cyanide.

Psychic surgery. It's big business in the Philippines and Brazil. Big show business, that is. Using sleight of hand and the gullibility of desperate patients, the practitioner pretends to reach inside a person's body and pull out a tumor (usually a raw animal part). With the deft aid of a squib or a fake thumb, blood appears to spill. The late comic Andy Kaufman resorted to psychic surgery in a last-ditch effort to cure his lung cancer.

Iscador. This is an extract of a European form of mistletoe, which was revered in ancient times and is still jokingly thought to bring luck to those who kiss under it at Christmas. Iscador is fermented and injected into the abdominal wall or directly into the tumor, based on the precepts of anthroposophy, a philosophy of balanced bodily forces invented in the early twentieth century by Rudolf Steiner. It is sold and administered mostly in Germany and

Switzerland. Studies of iscador continue to be carried out, but so far evidence is "weak and inconclusive," according to the Task Force on Alternative Therapies of the Canadian Breast Cancer Research Initiative. This is the treatment Suzanne Somers turned to, against the advice of her doctors, following a lumpectomy and radiation.

Hydrazine sulfate. The National Cancer Institute sponsored three clinical trials of this drug before declaring it ineffective in 1994. But it got unexpected publicity when Kathy Keeton, wife of *Penthouse* publisher Bob Guiccione, turned to it instead of chemotherapy when she was diagnosed with breast cancer in 1995. Sadly, Keeton died of metastatic breast cancer two years later, and her personal physician, Dr. Jeffrey Mechanic, reported that the tumor mass had not changed appreciably in either direction during that time.

NOW FOR THE GOOD NEWS

My dear friend Diane Stefani, who had two lumpectomies, sees an acupuncturist twice a month, a kickboxing trainer every week, a psychic every now and then, and a reflexologist when the mood strikes. She comes away from the acupuncture appointments with a goofy look of pure bliss. Even her voice seems different, like a kitten purring.

My friend Marie's mother, Teresa, is "a great believer in supplements. I've tried them all: Chiropractic, massage therapy, visualization, meditation—everything!"

Complementary therapies are generally harmless and can make you feel better. In some cases, they make you feel so good it can make all the difference in how you view and handle your medical treatments. Some therapies can open up new avenues of exploration that will continue to nourish body and spirit in years to come, long after you have finished dealing with breast cancer. Many people love these therapies so much they continue to practice them all their lives.

These therapies won't cure cancer (and don't claim to), but they can make medical treatment and daily quality of life infinitely more pleasurable, which in itself is an important component of healing. If they put your mind at ease, lower your blood pressure and heart rate, induce compliance with doctor's orders, help you sleep at night, give you a sense of replenishment and spiritual fulfillment, or make you feel that your body and energies are restored, then they're worth exploring. These are also therapies you can largely do for yourself (although I hope you won't try acupuncture on your own), and which can heighten the sense that you are taking control of your health.

"Complementary therapies are very different from alternative therapies, and they are what we offer here," says Dr. Cassileth. "They are not promoted as cancer cures. But they do deal with side effects, they do enhance quality of life, and they do a variety of very positive things."

The center offers therapies including body work (various forms of massage); spiritual therapies like meditation; creative therapies involving art, music, and sound; nutritional and herbal counseling; movement therapies such as yoga and tai chi, and such pain-relief methods as acupuncture, biofeedback, and hypnotherapy. "We are constantly adding and shifting according to what patients are interested in," says Cassileth. "We have found acupuncture remarkably effective for more than the lower back pain and the arthritis and nausea that the National Institutes of Health (NIH) consensus conference [in 1997] talked about. We found it very useful for fatigue. Many people find that it helps with depression and anxiety. It's a very idiosyncratic therapy."

Memorial Sloan-Kettering Cancer Center, once known as an icy palace of professional reserve, was one of the first cancer hospitals to offer these services to their patients. But just because these therapies are offered in a hospital setting doesn't mean they are completely understood. For example, the theory of why acupuncture works on some patients has changed over time. With acupuncture, invented by the Chinese, small needles are placed under the skin along "meridians" said to track energy flow. Acupuncture was invented before medicine knew what the inside of the body looked like, and one school of thought has it that meridians approximated what the Chinese glimpsed of the network of blood vessels from accident victims.

As science began to look into acupuncture, which is used with and sometimes instead of anesthesia in China, it was thought that the way it worked was by stimulating the body's endorphins, those natural chemicals that help block pain (it's known as "runner's high" when it kicks in during exercise). Now it is believed that acupuncture stimulates neurologic pressure points.

No matter the mechanism by which they work, complementary therapies are wildly popular in the United States. You won't find a more enthusiastic bunch than the people who swear by them. One would be hard-pressed to love surgery, but who doesn't like a massage?

Here's Teresa again, experimenter with "everything," who got a lottery-type windfall when she was asked to participate in a study on touch therapy at the University of Miami. For six weeks, she received a one-hour massage three times a week. For free! "You feel lighter, you feel happier, and you have a wonderful mental attitude after a good massage," she reports from the forefront of research. I have not conducted a double-blind test, but it is my personal belief that there's no downside to a series of free massages in the name of science.

Teresa also took up meditation toward the end of her breast-cancer treatments because, like many women, she was plagued by fears of fending for herself after all those months of medical surveillance. "Now I had to be on my own. What would happen to me? I did meditation for quite a few months, just to control whatever stress was developing. I sat outside in the garden, facing the ocean, and concentrated on my breath. For ten minutes, or even five, I think of nothing except doing my best. I always imagine myself in the percentage of people who survive."

Other people repeat a single word over and over to themselves (a mantra). Still others visualize their minds as having two windows, so that fleeting thoughts can come in and blow out again. One study showed that simply getting lost in the sounds of your favorite music was just as beneficial.

✳ YOGA

One of the first side effects of breast cancer kicked in the moment I was diagnosed and didn't let up for a long, long time. I called it the "mind race." My mind churned in *Star Trek*–like warp drive. If thinking alone burned calories I would have wasted away to nothing.

A lot of the mind race was taken up with worry. What's going to happen to me? Who will take care of my parrot? The mind race also yielded happy thoughts, albeit at full throttle. Aren't my friends great? Aren't birthdays a blast? Let's think up a few thousand things for my to-do list!

This humming, buzzing idea factory was getting annoying. Friends suggested yoga, and it just happens that I live in Yoga Central in New York where every other building seems to house an offshoot of some ancient school of tantric discipline. You can try yoga for the stretching, breathing, and relaxation exercises. Or you can subscribe to the idea that yoga puts you in good stead in the afterlife. Either way, if you go to a yoga class, you will find a sprinkling of breast-cancer survivors

who can be counted on to look for gently therapeutic methods of easing mind and body.

Yoga is so popular in New York it is practically a contact sport. Even beginners stand on
their heads, and you'd better hustle to find a
place for your sticky mat (to lie on) or else
some yogic bruiser will elbow you aside. As
the teacher announced which asana, or position, was next, the group murmured apprecia-
tively the way waiters sometimes flatter you
into thinking you've made the only sophisticated choice from the menu.

While the other students hung upside down
from ropes and bars like bats on the ceiling of
a cavern, the yoga teacher set me up with a
series of pillows and bolsters and a position
that would stretch my chest without causing
damage to the surgical area. All I needed was
a blanket and lights out and it would have
been perfect. Clearing the mind of all thoughts
is appropriate to the yogic discipline, but I was
unable to clear mine of one final thought: I
hoped the other students wouldn't step on me
in their zeal to get to the next asana.

POPULAR COMPLEMENTARY THERAPIES

Reflexology. A foot massage is a wonderful thing (unless you're really ticklish), and your local spa is not the first to discover it. There are pictographs of the ancient Egyptians getting foot massages.

The notion that specific zones on the foot are mystically allied with the internal organs was invented in the early 1900s and continues today with the popularity of reflexologists, who offer pressure-point massages, as opposed to the familiar rubbing type when you're trying to warm your feet. Believers imagine that a "life force" connects specific points on the foot to different parts of the body—the ball of the foot is supposedly allied with the chest area—and that interruptions in the flow of this energy can make people ill.

A reflexology treatment usually takes about half an hour. Like a pedicure, it can be very soothing and increase circulation to the feet. Avoid these massages if you have vascular problems in the lower legs.

Tai chi. This ancient Chinese set of body movements and postures has been popularized in the West by movies and pop culture. Along with Qigong, tai chi is known as an "internal martial art," one that's nourishing to the soul. This is not the kind of exercise where you karate-chop a pile of wood boards. Unlike the cultivation of physical strength, which relies on the building of muscles through weights and/or sports, tai chi tries to develop an inner sense of strength and balance that some breast-cancer patients find helpful for coping with treatment. It is taught at health clubs and more spiritual venues, but requires years of practice and dedication to get right.

Biofeedback. This technique helps you focus attention on your body to do such things as slow your heart rate, lower your blood pressure and relax. Many people use it to reduce stress and stress-related problems like headaches and depression.

As opposed to such passive therapies as massage and acupuncture, biofeedback requires you to participate and interact with the practitioner who is monitoring the session. Sensors are attached to parts of your body and signals from those points let you know whether you have been successful at a particular endeavor, like slowing the heart rate or influencing other bodily functions that are usually automatic.

One of the lures of biofeedback for breast-cancer patients is that it gives them a feeling of hands-on control over their bodies.

Do not try this if you have a pacemaker or heart problems, as a small amount of electricity is generated by the machines measuring your responses.

Chiropractic. The theory behind this popular treatment is that "subluxations" impede the flow of "Innate Intelligence" through the body, and that it can all be straightened out by manipulating ("adjusting") the spine. So far, studies have shown that chiropractic may help relieve temporary lower back pain, the kind of pain that is self-limiting and will go away by itself in time. Adherents believe the manipulation, usually done in a number of sessions over several weeks, hastens the recovery process and restores full range to joints and muscles.

During these treatments, the chiropractor relieves pressure on certain joints, resulting in the "popping" sound you hear when cracking your knuckles. While breast cancer is not a musculoskeletal disease, and therefore would not seem to be a likely candidate for spinal manipulation, nearly anyone subjected to the stress of such a diagnosis could experience the occasional lower-back twinge.

Macrobiotic diet. We discussed earlier how breast-cancer patients often turn to more restrictive diet plans, like vegetarianism, in hope of avoiding recurrence. While no combination of foods can cure cancer, a diet low in fat and high in fiber is consistent with good health and what we know of cancer prevention.

Macrobiotics is a more severe form of vegetarianism. It is based on old Chinese ideas about the yin and yang of a body in balance. The strict, nutritionally arbitrary rules of macrobiotics may deprive you of vital nourishment while you're going through breast-cancer treatments, so if you follow such a regimen, be sure to ask your doctor what vitamin supplements, if any, to take.

Creative therapies: Art, writing, and music are all activities that help patients come to terms with their breast cancer. They are creative, cathartic endeavors, and you needn't feel you have any talent before trying them. Many people find that keeping a journal is extremely helpful, not only for expressing your feelings of the moment, but as a map of how far you've traveled through the experience. Many cancer organizations offer such workshops, where the emphasis is on making sense of your experience rather than selling your work and going on talk shows.

10

Getting Back to Normal

I remember prancing out of the hospital on my last day of radiation. I had tons of plans, specific ones for the rest of the day and vague ones for the rest of my life. But finishing treatment and getting back to "normal" are not the same thing, and it was not as simple as I had thought.

First of all, there's no "normal." Not after having breast cancer. In any case, my life is not the same as it was before cancer, but then, it wasn't my goal to put everything back exactly the way it was. I have a new concept of "normal," a life that is enhanced by what I learned about myself in the course of becoming a breast-cancer survivor.

Both your mind and body will need TLC after treatments end, although there's no set time period for how long it will take for you to feel fully healed. One woman told me she only began feeling free of chemo's traces three years later. Teresa, whom we last met meditating on the beach, said it took her eight to nine months after chemo and radiation to feel like herself physically, although she snapped right back psychologically. Everyone who has had cancer must grapple with some physical and psychological residue for a time, and all of us still suffer the occasional dark night of the soul, those 3 A.M. jitters when we wonder just how safe we are.

There is no set deadline for "total" recovery. One woman I know says she still cries at night and remains fearful. Another feels fine now, but her equanimity depends on not revisiting Cancer World in either thought or conversation. Yet another is working at rebuilding her life, just as she is remodeling her house. We all have to keep at it to find through trial and error what works for us.

On the physical front, chemo and/or radiation are very harsh on the system. Your treatments may end, but it can be just the beginning of reclaiming your strength. This is the first book I'm daring to write since I finished treatments, because it's the first time I trust that I have the energy to see it through.

In general, the younger and better shape you're in, the faster you'll spring back, but stories abound of feeling draggy and not quite right for a long time afterward. One woman from my support group says the word "chemo" as if she is uttering a curse word, whereas a woman from a different support group says she was afraid the chemo didn't work because she never felt tired.

The difficulty inherent in "getting back to normal" is

not only physical, but a function of realizing, geez! I just came *thisclose*!

This is not meant to frighten you. The mere fact that you're considering how you'll feel afterward is a luxury that at one time you weren't sure you'd have. The minute you find yourself planning a future, then you know you're back on the road to "normal."

I realized this the day I took out a five-year subscription to *Consumer Reports*. Not a one-year subscription, but a five-year subscription, and don't think it was easy! Looking forward involves making a lot of overlapping plans that involve different time frames—maybe a five-year plan for money you want to save or a career you want to have, maybe a six-month plan for getting back in shape. Making a lunch date with a friend for next week is a wonderful start. Life goes on, and your focus will gradually widen from a life composed of connecting the dots of your doctor appointments to a life that's full of love, laughter, and really bad reality-TV shows. It's all there for you when you're ready for it.

There's a certain amount of adapting you have to do. Just because the doctor says, "You're fine! Go home!," does not mean you feel fine that day, and that your life will pick up exactly as before. Just as when recovering from an accident, you need to find your pace and slowly add things back in. Even if you are itching for a *Guinness Book* entry's worth of activity, you may have misjudged your still-tender emotions.

Here's some good news. Almost everyone I know who has had breast cancer says she feels better for the experience. That will translate to a fuller, richer life only if you want it to, and if you're willing to work at it. You can use your cancer experience as a springboard to make changes in your life. Or you can just go back to what you were doing before, more or less. Despite what people think, you don't wake up each day with a yelp of glee any more than any person does. The novelty of surviving wears off, and life goes on.

In the years since my treatment I have kept a list of things I love and slowly brought them back into my life. I began with swim aerobics classes twice a week, because I love water and I needed the exercise. Swimming is the gentlest activity next to bingo, and there were many people (mostly women) in the class who were either pregnant, recovering from injury, or not flexible enough to do certain exercises on dry land. I told my instructor that I had to be careful about injuring my left arm, and she always looked out for me during stretches or difficult maneuvers.

After a year, I added skiing lessons. It turns out I have something bordering on a fetish for snow. I get an immense sense of well-being when I see snow, walk in it, or even think about it. So I took beginner's ski lessons and stayed as long as needed on the bunny slope to feel confident.

My legs were getting stronger from the skiing, so I decided that, even though I was terrified, I wanted to ride horses. I've always wanted to ride horses. Am I not a female? So I took lessons, gradually got over many of my fears (height, speed, stepping in manure). I am now the proud owner of a pair of genuine paddock boots.

It was an easy leap from there to buying a bicycle, getting a driver's license (don't ask why it took so long), and more. I read in bed before I go to sleep, a pleasure left over from childhood. I take bubble baths with aromatic unguents. After a year of being wrapped up in medical treatments, where cancer was all I could think about, I became a pleasure machine! I bought plants for my patio because they please my eye, I went back (finally) to lifting weights because I enjoy having muscles, I read books on any and every topic to see what else in the world I might be missing in the way of information and ideas. It's a full and wonderful life, and I'm enjoying myself immensely.

Before cancer, I was a workaholic. There was no time for baths and waxing my skis. So, no, I am not back to normal, I am never going back to normal, and I am much happier for it.

Tip: Friends and loved ones will feel relieved when your treatments are done because they believe they can stop worrying about you. But you will not feel any immediate difference just because treatments end. In fact, you may find yourself depressed as you near the finish of your treatments, or on the one-year anniversary of your diagnosis. Just because you're "finished" doesn't mean it's over for you emotionally.

WAYS TO EASE THE POST-CANCER TRANSITION

- **Fasten your seat belt.** Family members may have bottled up their feelings during your illness, and they may still need an outlet for their fear and anxiety. The most common such outlet is the sudden, seemingly inexplicable argument.

- **Look to the little ones.** Children especially may continue to feel frightened for you or for themselves. Give them extra attention and reassurance, and leave the door open to talking about it if and when they want to.

- **Ask for help.** Don't be ashamed of seeking professional counseling. The period directly after cancer treatments can be emotionally fraught in ways you'd never expect.

- **Take the high road.** Get to work on those relationships that you want to preserve. Some people, including your spouse or significant other, may have withdrawn during your treatments, but not necessarily for the evil reasons you fear. It could be that they felt helpless or confused and weren't sure how to give you what you needed. Reach out to them, and don't give up on them.

- **Sex doesn't have to sizzle.** Resuming sexual relations either during or after treatments can provoke anxiety, especially if you have post-surgery body image problems. If chemo has put you into menopause, you may also be experiencing vaginal dryness, for which there are water-soluble lubricants at the pharmacy. But nothing beats taking it slow and getting to know your partner all over again.

- **Use protection.** Even if your period seems to have stopped because of chemo, be careful. Your body has been bombarded with chemicals and your resistance may still be low. You'll want to be especially careful not to get pregnant if you are continuing on tamoxifen.

✳ BREAST-CANCER "SURVIVOR"

There are plenty of women who reject the term "survivor" and are more comfortable thinking of themselves in other ways, using other terms. My friend Marguerite, an artist who has a gorgeous rose trellis tattoo on her chest over the mastectomy scar, objects to the military overtones of the term.

Laura,* who had thyroid cancer at age twenty-three and breast cancer a few years ago, prefers to call herself an endurer. She quotes *Webster's*: "To endure is 'to remain firm under suffering or misfortune without yielding.' To survive is 'to continue to live or exist after.' 'Survivor' seems to accentuate the negative. I prefer to acknowledge my strength.

---

*Yes, this is the Laura who gave me my hamster when I was nine. I know you'll want to keep track of this sort of thing.

I believe I now live at a superior level through my experiences."

I admit there is something a little weird about the term "survivor." It makes us sound either as if we did something heroic or just sat the whole thing out stoically. You have to find a way to think about your experience that feels comfortable to you, and you are free to reject the pigeonholes and sound-bite explanations the general culture offers.

STAYING CONNECTED

After your treatments, you may think you never want to spend a second's thought on cancer again. But most women like to keep up some kind of connection with this thing that forever more will be a major chunk of their personal history.

Some people stay on in support groups after treatments end, or seek solace from groups with which they have more in common, such as the Young Survival Web site (www.youngsurvival.org) dedicated to the experiences of women in their twenties and thirties. Some continue to talk things out in other ways, for example, through the Breast Cancer Listserv group on the Internet.

Donna Robbins volunteers at her former support group. "When I was going through it, I was one person. As a volunteer, I'm another person," she says. "It's strange, curious. Now I realize that all the little stuff was not important, and I used to be a worrywart over every stupid little thing. Having breast cancer really relieved me of that. My priorities are better since then. I think I enjoy life more now, maybe because I worry less."

Musa Mayer, a contributing editor at MAMM magazine (for women with breast or reproductive cancers), has written about her breast cancer. Like all authors, she knows the value of catharsis through the written word, and she shares that knowledge in Writing Our Way Home workshops, where women put thoughts about their experience on paper.

Another way to stay connected, while helping the cause at the same time, is by participating in an annual event like the Race for the Cure, which is sponsored in many major cities by the Susan G. Komen Foundation. This three-mile race raises money for breast-cancer research. You sign up and have your friends "sponsor" you for the event, each contributing a certain amount if you finish the race.

And don't presume you have to be a marathon runner to complete three miles. My first time on the course was while I was still in chemo, and I was hot, tired, whiny, and slow. I called it the "Trudge for the Cure." When I crossed the finish line the announcer boomed, "And here comes another *survivor!*" It brought tears to my eyes, then and now.

If you're up for it, there's Avon's Breast Cancer 3-Day, which is a three-day, fifty-mile walk that includes camping out overnight. Avon provides the tents, meals, snacks, drinks, Porta-Sans, blister cream, and even a few massages at the end of the day. It is one of the most moving experiences you'll ever have.

My friend Meg used to telephone me often during treatment and ask whether I was "horizontal" or "vertical" that day. She promised that every year we were both vertical, we would run (or trudge) the Race for the Cure together. We have finished four of the races so far, each of them at our own pace, in our own time.

✳ KICKING THE SLEEPING-PILL HABIT

You read elsewhere in this book how I turned to a prescription drug to help me get a decent night's rest during cancer treatments. I had come to be jealous of people suffering from sleep apnea—at least *they* got a few seconds of sleep between snores! Me, I was awake and wild-eyed at four in the morning. Half or even a third of a gentle sleeping pill solved the problem.

And it created a new one. I couldn't fall asleep without it, not even after my cancer treatments ended. It was time to get the monkey off my back.

After much research, I have discovered one

possible cure for returning to natural, deep sleep. You have to go somewhere really high up. The higher the altitude, the less oxygen in the air. Your best bet is Mount Everest, where you pass out right away from oxygen deprivation, then write a best-seller about the experience.

But Everest is expensive, so any high altitude will do. Check out the ski resorts. Ah! There's nothing like a little hypoxia to lull you into slumberland.

CHANGING YOUR LIFE . . . OR NOT

"My experience is that most people do not change their lives radically after treatment," says Roz Kleban, who runs the support group at Memorial Sloan-Kettering Cancer Center. "While they're going through it, they feel they will never ever be the same, but the good news is they *will* be the same!"

You can elect to change your life after breast cancer, and those who have done so report it as being very positive. "I think it has improved the quality of my life," says Teresa, our seaside meditator. "I'm more aware and conscious of things than before breast cancer. I think I am more humane, more compassionate. Overall, I'm a better human being nowadays."

Teresa also has a new career, thanks to breast cancer—the former aviation consultant now spends 90 percent of her work life as a volunteer at the Miami branch of the National Breast Cancer Coalition. "I was handling it well psychologically and emotionally, so I decided to do something to fight breast cancer. I called several organizations, and found I was more in tune with this one. We're activists who deal with politicians in Washington. Our main goal is to raise federal funds for breast-cancer research. But besides that, we have legislation we want to pass in Congress to favor women with breast cancer. It's a very powerful organization. I joined them during my chemo, learned to deal with politicians, and now I'm the group's legislative chair."

Teresa thinks that although the finer points of her transformation are unique, the outcome is typical. "You can turn a negative experience into a positive outcome. That's what I tried to do from the first—fight this monster and also do something to eradicate it. I am grateful that I have the privilege of being able to help other people. Helping them has enlightened me."

Kleban says that if your life changes after cancer, "it's because you worked at making a positive change." And even if it doesn't, no harm done. "This is not an experience that will diminish your life," says Kleban. "It can enhance your life. While you're being treated, everything you feel, you feel exquisitely. There's an intensity of feeling. During that period, your feelings are tremendously enhanced."

ONE FINAL WORD

Breast cancer, from diagnosis through treatment and well beyond, is complicated on so many levels. One of the many reasons for the comparative rosiness of my recollections today is my intense gratitude for having survived it all, or at least having survived it all for now. With the benefit of hindsight, it is easy for me to gloss over some of the pain, dread, and hassle of that year. At the same time, today's rosy view is balanced by yesterday's troughs of despair. During my layover in Cancer World, it was nearly impossible to appreciate the bigger picture, including how blessedly fortunate I was—and so are you, reading this book—to have today. It's really all we can ask for, and it is no little thing.

Suggested Reading

A lot of the research for this book was done on the Internet, because that's just the way the world works now. But we must never lose the joy of curling up with a good book. Here are a few I consulted. Some are strictly about breast cancer. Others are on tangential topics, but you might want to read them just for fun:

The Alternative Medicine Handbook, by Barrie R. Cassileth, Ph.D. (Norton, 1997). One of the few trustworthy guides through the thicket of alternative claims.

Beauty & Cancer: Looking and Feeling Your Best, by Diane Doan Noyes and Peggy Mellody, R.N. (Taylor Publishing, 1992). Illustrated guide to tying turbans and putting on makeup to disguise the effects of cancer treatments.

Cute, Quaint, Hungry, and Romantic: The Aesthetics of Consumerism, by Daniel Harris (Basic Books, 2000). Sophisticated critique of our culture, including the ways that unhealthy things are marketed to seem enticing.

Dr. Susan Love's Breast Book, 3rd Edition, by Susan

Love (Perseus, 2000). A one-stop resource by a doctor who is passionate on the subject.

An Encylopedia of Claims, Frauds, and Hoaxes of the Occult and Supernatural, by James Randi (St. Martins, 1995). An entertaining A to Z of quackery, including many cancer-cure scams throughout the ages.

Everyone's Guide to Cancer Therapy, 3rd Edition, by Malin Dollinger, M.D., Ernest H. Rosenbaum, M.D., and Greg Cable (Andrews McMeel, 1998). Highly readable guide to many kinds of cancer, including breast cancer.

The Faith Healers, by James Randi (Prometheus, 1987). More on medical charlatanism; you'll never be fooled again.

The Health Robbers: A Close Look at Quackery in America, edited by Stephen Barrett, M.D., and William T. Jarvis, Ph.D. (Prometheus, 1993). Meticulous and fascinating compendium of research into modern medical quackery.

A History of the Breast, by Marilyn Yalom (Ballantine Books, 1997). A well-researched study of how the breast has been perceived culturally, including a chapter on the history of our understanding of breast disease.

Home Comforts, by Cheryl Mendelson (Scribner, 1999). Terrific and surprisingly soothing bedside reading about the art and science of keeping house. In the interests of insomniacs and breast-cancer patients who need a place to recharge their batteries, I consulted the section on how to make your bed the most enticing place in the world.

Losing It: False Hopes and Fat Profits in the Diet Indus-

try, by Laura Fraser (Penguin, 1998). This book happily bursts the bubble of diet scams.

My Breast: One Woman's Cancer Story, by Joyce Wadler (Pocket Books, 1992). One of the best (and funniest) memoirs of a painful time, by a *New York Times* reporter with a gift for the telling detail.

Stedman's Medical Dictionary, 27th Edition, by Thomas Lathrop Stedman (Williams & Wilkins, 2000). Not exactly light reading, but an excellent resource.

Why People Believe Weird Things, by Michael Shermer (Freeman, 1997). This book, though not about cancer, will help you learn critical thinking so as not to be seduced by false medical claims.

Resources

American Cancer Society/Breast Cancer Network
    Write to:
    1559 Clifton Road, NE
    Atlanta, GA 30329, or
    Call: 1-800-227-2345, or
    Visit their Web site at http://www2.cancer.org/bcn/
        inex.html
        This solid, practical, and reliable site not only pro-
        vides information and other resources, it includes
        survivor stories.

American Institute for Cancer Research
    Write to:
    1759 R Street, NW
    Washington, DC 20009, or
    Call: 1-800-843-8114, or
    Visit their Web site at http://www.aicr.org
        The Institute offers details on helping to prevent
        cancer through nutrition and diet, from newslet-
        ters to cookbooks.

American Medical Association
Visit their Web site at: http://www.ama-assn.org/ insight/spec-con/breast/brc.htm
This site describes the warning signs of breast cancer, as well as offering instruction on how to perform a breast self-examination (BSE). You can also search for doctors and review their credentials at http://www.ama-assn.org

Breast Cancer and Environmental Risk Factors Project
Visit their Web site at http://www.cfe.cornell. edu/bcerf
This site provides fact sheets, critical evaluations, bibliographies, and a searchable database on breast cancer and environmental risk factors.

Breast Cancer Answers
Visit their Web site at http://www.medsch.wisc. edu/bca
This is a service of the University of Wisconsin Comprehensive Cancer Center, providing reliable and up-to-date information on prevention, detection, diagnosis, staging, and treatment, as well as research.

Breast Cancer Awareness
Visit their Web site at http://www.tricaresw.af.mil/ breastcd/index.html
This interactive site from the U.S. Department of Defense TRICARE provides useful information on a broad range of issues concerning breast health.

Breast Cancer Online
Visit their Web site at http://www.bco.org
This is an independent educational service and source of information for professionals working in the field of breast cancer. It includes conference information and reports, news, links, case studies, and questions for self-assessment.

Buddy Program for Breast Cancer Clinical Trials
Visit their Web site at http://www.gis.net/~allisonm/buddies.html
This program links women who are eligible for a breast cancer clinical trial with a trained "buddy"—a woman who has been in a similar trial and can tell about her experience.

Cancer Care, Inc.
Write to:
275 Seventh Avenue
New York, NY 10001, or
Call: 1-800-813-4673, or
Visit their Web site at: http://www.cancercare.org
They offer free counseling, support groups, and seminars, as well as referrals and other information.

Cancer Research Foundation of America
Write to:
1600 Duke Street, Suite 110
Alexandria, VA 22314, or
Call: 1-800-227-CRFA, or

Visit their Web site at: http://www.preventcancer.org
This foundation offers information on preventing cancer through lifestyle changes, as well as other information, including special events.

Community Breast Health Project
Visit their Web site at http://www-med.stanford.edu/CBHP/
This site offers breast-cancer information to patients and survivors of breast cancer. It includes practical advice and links to other Web sites that have breast cancer information.

ENCORE
Write to:
Office of Women's Health Initiatives
624 Ninth Street, NW
Washington, DC 20001, or
Call: 202-628-3636, or
Visit their Web site at http://www.ywca.org
This is the YWCA's discussion and exercise program for women who have had breast cancer surgery. It is designed to help restore physical strength and emotional well-being.

Gilda's Club
Write to:
195 West Houston Street
New York, NY 10014, or
Call: 212-647-9700, or

Fax: 212-647-1151, or

Visit their Web site at http://www.gildasclub.org

This nonprofit organization offers its services free of charge to people with cancer, their families, and friends. Its mission is to provide a place where people unite for mutual support that complements medical care. Services include networking groups, lectures, workshops, and social events in a comfortable and friendly environment. With twenty-five branches nationally and more planned, it offers classes in meditation, healthy cooking, tai chi, and has facilities for children.

Inflammatory Breast Cancer Research Foundation

Visit their Web site at http://www.ibcresearch.org

This Web site is dedicated to the advancement of research on inflammatory breast cancer.

Living Beyond Breast Cancer

Write to:

10 East Athens Avenue, Suite 204

Ardmore, PA 19003, or

Call: 1-888-753-5222, or

Visit their Web site at: http://www.lbbc.org

This organization disseminates information from and offers referrals to other resources, including self-help groups.

Look Good, Feel Better
  Call 1-800-395-LOOK, or
  Call the American Cancer Society at 1-800-227-2345.
    This organization offers free makeup along with a
    free class on how to apply it, plus tips for counter-
    acting the side effects of treatment on appearance.

MAMM Magazine
  Write to:
  349 West 12th St.
  New York, NY 10014-1796, or
  Call: 1-888-901-MAMM
  Or send e-mail to subscription@mamm.com
    An uplifting, informative, and very well-written
    magazine for women with breast or reproductive
    cancer. And I'm not just saying these nice things
    because I happen to write for them . . . although I
    hope you'll read my column, Cancer Girl, which
    deals with aspects of cancer with humor.

Medscape
  Visit their Web site at http://www.medscape.com
    This Web site offers truly detailed, reliable infor-
    mation. Health-care professionals frequently log
    on, but it's also useful for the interested consumer.
    There's a searchable database of peer-reviewed ar-
    ticles, and a database called DrugSearch where you
    can look up the drugs you're taking or the side ef-
    fects you're experiencing.

The National Alliance of Breast Cancer Organizations
Write to:
9 East 37 Street
New York, NY 10016, or
Call: 1-888-806-2226, or
Visit their Web site at http://www.nabco.org/
> NABCO is a coalition of more than 370 organizations that provide breast cancer detection, treatment, and care to thousands of women. The Web site provides information on clinical trials, a resource router to cancer information resources on the Internet, and links to local breast cancer support groups.

National Breast Cancer Coalition
Write to:
1707 L Street, NW, Suite 1060
Washington, DC 20036, or
Call: 202-296-7477, or
Visit their Web site at http://www.natlbcc.org/
> This organization focuses on increasing research, increasing access for all women to quality treatment and clinical trials, and increasing the influence in Congress of women living with breast cancer.

National Cancer Institute (CancerNet)
Write to:
NCI Public Inquiries Office
Bldg 31, Rm 10A03
31 Center Drive, MSC 2580
Bethesda, MD 20892-2580, or
Call: 1-800-422-6237, or
Visit their Web site at http://www.cancernet.nci.nih.gov
CancerNet provides a wealth of information, and
on its Web site you can have that information for-
matted for the layperson or the health professional.
The Web site lists ongoing clinical trials, as well as
statistics and treatment broken down by cancer
stage.

National Coalition for Cancer Survivorship
Write to:
1010 Wayne Avenue, Suite 770
Silver Springs, MD 20910-5600, or
Call: 877-622-7937, or
Visit their Web site at: http://www.cansearch.org
The coalition has resources on-line and sponsors
conferences and other events.

National Council for Reliable Health Information
(NCRHI)
Visit their Web site at http://www.ncrhi.org
An important organization with chapters nation-
wide, devoted to educating consumers, profession-
als, and the government about health deceptions

and quackery. Formerly known as the National Council Against Health Fraud. Includes a list of medically reliable Web sites that have been vetted by professionals.

The National Lymphedema Network (NLN)
    Write to:
    2211 Post Street, Suite 404
    San Francisco, CA 94115-3427, or
    Call 1-800-541-3259 or 415-921-1306, or
    Visit their Web site at http://www.lymphnet.org
        This support organization for women experiencing swelling of the arm as a result of lymph node removal was founded by a registered nurse and can refer patients to local treatment facilities. To learn more about lymphedema, contact: the American Cancer Society (see above), or the National Cancer Institute (NCI) at http://www.cancernet.nci.nih.gov/clinpdq/supportive_pat/Lymphedema_Patient.html, or OncoLink at http://www.oncolink.com/support/lymphedema

Oncolink
    Visit their Web site at http://www.oncolink.com
        Offered by the University of Pennsylvania, this monster site covers financial issues as well as offering good basic information on screening and prevention.

QuackWatch
   Visit the Web site at http://www.quackwatch.com
      A must Web site if you're thinking of trying alternative medicine, or don't know whom to trust. This extensive, well-researched site addresses all manner of health fraud, including on the Internet. There's even a "Special Message for Cancer Patients Seeking Alternative Treatment" site listed on the home page, and resources for recommended and non-recommended reading.

Reach to Recovery Program
   Visit their Web site at http://www2.cancer.org/bcn/reach.html
      This program of the American Cancer Society has been helping patients with breast cancer cope with their diagnosis, treatment, and recovery since 1952, with survivor-to-patient outreach and support. Originally a service for women still in the hospital after their mastectomies, it now supports women from diagnosis through treatment.

Scientific Review of Alternative Medicine
   Write to:
   Quackwatch
   P.O. Box 1747
   Allentown, PA 18105
      This highly readable quarterly publication is the only peer-reviewed journal to analyze the claims of alternative and complementary treatments objec-

tively. Past issues have included analyses of nutritional claims for curing cancer and whether prayer promotes healing. This is the real deal.

The Susan G. Komen Breast Cancer Foundation
Write to:
5005 LBJ Freeway, Suite 250
Dallas, TX 75244, or
E-mail concerns about breast health to helpline@komen.org, or
E-mail requests for educational material to education@komen.org, or
E-mail for information about the Race for the Cure to raceforthecure@komen.org, or
Call: 1-800-462-9273, or
Fax: 972-855-1605, or
Visit their Web site at http://www.komen.org
Another Web site that is a service of this foundation is http://www.breastcancerinfo.com.
Widely known for their sponsorship of the fundraising Race for the Cure, the foundation also offers survivor stories and other news and information.

Tessin, LLC
Call: 1-800-480-8608, or
Fax: 203-366-1619, or
E-mail: dtessin@tessin.net, or
Visit their Web site at: http://www.tessin.net
This company sells comfort. Their specialty is

Night Sweats, a bed linen that is made of natural cotton terry velour. It's highly absorbent, which is important for women who experience night sweats and hot flashes, which can be side effects of chemo and tamoxifen.

Women's Cancer Network
Write to:
c/o Gynecologic Cancer Foundation
401 North Michigan Avenue
Chicago, IL 60611, or
Call: 312-644-6610, or
Visit their Web site at: http://www.wcn.org
This site includes methods of calculating your risk for cancer, as well as ways to get books and referrals.

Y-ME National Breast Cancer Organization
Write to:
212 West Van Buren, 5th Floor
Chicago, IL 60607-3907, or
Call (English): 1-800-221-2141, or
Call (Spanish): 1-800-986-9505, or
E-mail: info@y-me.org, or
Visit their Web site at http://www.y-me.org
A hotline is staffed by trained counselors who have had breast cancer and who provide information and support as well as access to a variety of resources, twenty-four hours a day. Trained male counslors are also available to talk to male partners of breast can-

cer patients. Y-me attempts to match callers by diagnosis and treatment type, upon request. For women with limited financial resources, their Wig and Prosthesis Bank will mail these items for a minimal handling fee. Y-me's home page includes breast health information, breast self-examination (BSE) guidelines, a Kid's Corner, newsletters, publication ordering information, and "Ask Y-ME," a unique opportunity to have questions answered quickly and confidentially. They also have a Teen Program to introduce high-school girls to breast health awareness.

GLOSSARY

A

ablation: A term meaning to eradicate, obliterate. You may hear this term used in reference to bone marrow that has been wiped out due to chemo or radiation, or surgically, as in ovarian ablation, where the ovaries are removed or treated to effectively halt the production of estrogen.

abscess: A collection of pus, usually caused by bacterial infection. The pus is formed by dead white blood cells after they have attacked the bacteria at the infection site. If it occurs in the breast, a doctor should be consulted.

absolute neutrophil count: A tally of neutrophils, particles that normally make up more than half of all white blood cells (WBC), that is determined by multiplying the percentage of neutrophils by total WBC count. An ANC of 2,000–1,000 is mildly neutrophenic. See also **neutrophils.**

adenocarcinoma: A cancerous (malignant) tumor

that involves cells from the lining of the walls of many different bodily organs, and which excrete mucous or other substances. Breast cancer is a type of adenocarcinoma.

adjuvant treatment: Additional treatment that is administered for the purpose of extending or enhancing the effects of a primary treatment. In breast cancer, adjuvant therapy may entail chemo, hormone therapy, and/or radiation therapy.

alkylating agents: A class of chemo drugs that attack tumor cells during the resting and dividing stages.

alopecia: Hair loss, which can be a temporary result of some chemotherapy.

ambulatory: Able to get out of bed and walk around. This term is used especially after surgery.

amenorrhea (menostasis): The cessation of menstrual periods, sometimes induced by chemo. Breast cancer patients often refer to it as "chemo-pause."

analgesic (analgetic): A medicine given to control or reduce pain. Common analgesics are aspirin, acetaminophen (which is less irritating to the stomach), and ibuprofen.

anaphylactic shock: Severe, sometimes fatal allergic reaction to the injection of a foreign substance. Anaphylaxis is an emergency condition whose symptoms include a sharp drop in blood pressure, breathing difficulty, and tachycardia (rapid and weak pulse).

anemia: A condition in which there are abnormally low levels of red blood cells. Chemo destroys red blood cells, so it is a common possible side effect. Symptoms include fatigue, dizziness, light-headedness, shortness of breath, difficulty staying warm, and chest pains.

anesthesia: The partial or total loss of sensation caused by disease, injury, acupuncture, or anesthetics (see below).

anesthetic: A group of drugs that causes entire or partial loss of feeling or sensation. They are commonly used before a painful procedure, such as surgery. Local anesthetics cause the loss of sensation only to the injected area. General anesthetics cause loss of consciousness as well as loss of sensation.

anorexia: Loss of appetite, especially as a result of a disease like cancer.

antiemetic: A drug that prevents or relieves nausea and vomiting, used during and sometimes after chemotherapy. It can be administered through an IV, or taken in pill or suppository form.

antimetabolites: A class of anticancer drugs that prohibits cell division by masquerading as nutrients to gain access to the cell.

antineoplastics: See **antitumor antibiotics**.

antioxidants: Chemical agents that inhibit damage caused by oxygen. These are found in certain foods and also produced by the body. They include vitamins C and

E, and beta-carotene (a form of vitamin A). They protect against free radicals, which are chemicals that alter molecular structure in a process called oxidation.

antitumor (anticancer, antineoplastic) antibiotics: A class of chemo agents that insert themselves into strands of DNA. They work by breaking up the chromosomes of the cell, or by preventing the DNA-dependent synthesis of RNA that the cells need to grow.

apoptosis: Cell death that is genetically programmed, or in the case of chemo and radiation, cell death induced by injury to cellular DNA. Also called cell suicide.

areola: Usually refers to the darker pigmented skin surrounding the nipple, textured by the glands underneath (areola mammae).

aspiration: Removal of fluid or small amount of cells by inserting a needle into a lump and drawing the fluid into the syringe. The purpose of the aspiration is to determine whether the lump is a fluid-filled cyst (noncancerous) or a solid mass (possibly cancerous).

asymptomatic: Without any sign of disease. Cancer in its early stages often exhibits no obvious symptoms.

autologous: Coming from the same person. In blood transfusion or in such procedures as **autologous bone marrow transplant,** the donor's own blood is stored in case she needs it.

autologous bone marrow transplant: A bone marrow transplant in which the donor is also the recipient. Bone marrow can be removed before a treatment like chemo, to be given back to the patient following treatment. The benefit of any autologous procedure is that it avoids the risk of rejection.

axilla: The underarm or armpit.

axillary (lymph node) dissection: The surgical removal of a portion of the lymph nodes under the arm so that the tissue may be examined for the spread of cancer.

B

benign tumor: Abnormal growth that is not cancerous and will not invade nearby tissue or spread to other parts of the body.

bilateral: Both sides of the body. Bilateral breast cancer means the cancer is in both breasts.

biological response modifier (hematopoietic growth factors, colony stimulating factors): A group of agents administered to patients with low blood counts to stimulate bone marrow production. Examples are Epogen, Procrit, and Neupogen. See also **biotherapy.**

biopsy: The removal of tissue surgically, or by aspiration, for diagnostic purposes. Excisional biopsy refers to a complete removal of a lump, and incision biopsy refers to a partial removal.

biotherapy (biological therapy, also known as **immunotherapy** or **biological response modifier therapy):**

Treatments that stimulate the immune system to ward off infection and disease. See also **biological response modifier.**

blood count: See **complete blood count.**

bone marrow: The soft, fatty tissue that fills the cavities of the bones (especially long bones), and that produces blood cells. Since chemotherapy affects the bone marrow, the number of red and white cells and platelets in the blood will decrease.

bone marrow biopsy and aspiration: A procedure in which a needle is used to retrieve a small amount of marrow from the center of a bone (usually the hip) for later examination. See **biopsy.**

bone scan: A screening procedure in which a trace amount of a radioactive substance is injected into the bloodstream so that the bones, and especially abnormalities therein, appear more distinctly in images. Its purpose is to see whether the cancer has spread there.

boost: The last few sessions of radiation therapy specifically administered to the original tumor site, and not across the whole breast area.

brachytherapy: See **internal radiation.**

BRCA-1: The gene found on chromosome 17 that normally regulates cell growth. Women with mutated versions of this gene have been found to have an increased, inherited risk of developing breast and ovarian cancer. Abnormalities in the gene BRCA-2, on chromosome 13, have also been associated with increased risk of breast cancer.

breast: See **mammary glands**.

breast cancer: A malignancy that originates in the breast. This cancer is potentially fatal if left unchecked or untreated. It affects both women and men, but is rare in men. See also **cancer.**

breast implant: Surgical reconstruction of the breast following a mastectomy using a sac filled with saline to restore shape. Since 1992, the FDA has imposed severe restrictions on the use of silicone in implants.

breast self-examination (BSE): A self-examination with the fingertips that should be done once a month for detection of changes in the breasts. The best recommended time to perform the BSE is after your period, when there is less tenderness and swelling in the breast.

C

calcifications: See **microcalcifications.**

cancer: A general term used to describe more than a hundred different uncontrolled growths of abnormal cells in the body. Cancer cells have the ability to continue to grow, invade, and destroy surrounding tissue, then travel to other parts of the body where they can set up new cancerous tumors.

cancer cell: A cell in the body that reproduces and

divides in an uncontrolled manner. Unlike normal cells, their growth is not regulated, and may result in an abnormal growth (see **neoplasm**) or may break away to remote parts of the body (see **metastasis**).

capsular contracture: A condition in which a firm, fibrous scar that forms around a breast implant thickens and constricts the area.

carcinogen: Any substance or organism that is known to cause, produce, or promote the development of cancer. Examples of carcinogens are tobacco and asbestos.

carcinoma: The most commonly occurring form of cancer. It grows in the tissue that lines such organs as the breast, and has a tendency to invade surrounding tissue.

carcinoma in situ: A carcinoma that is still confined to the site of origin. It is an early stage of development where it is highly curable.

CAT scan (computerized axial tomography, computed tomography, CT scan): An image of the body in cross sections generated by a computer from data obtained from X-ray transmission. These images can indicate the presence of cancer or metastasis.

catheter (also known as **central vascular access catheter**)**:** A tube implanted in the body to provide access to the bloodstream or a body cavity. It is sometimes used to administer chemo, thus avoiding using a needle each time. See also **vascular access device**.

cell differentiation: The stage in a cell's normal development in which it takes on specific, function-oriented characteristics. See also **differentiation**.

cellulitis: Inflammation of soft tissue. Breast-cancer patients who have had lymph node dissection are at greater risk of cellulitis as a result of infection at the surgery site.

chemotherapy: The use of chemical agents to combat cancer.

chromosomes: These contain genetic information found in the nucleus of the cell.

chronic: A health-related condition or disease that lasts or develops over a long period of time.

clavicle: Medical term for the collarbone.

clinical trial: An experiment in which the patient is a voluntary subject of research and treatment that has yet to be approved by the FDA.

colony-stimulating factors: Substances which encourage the production of blood cells, and which may be employed during chemotherapy or radiation therapy when certain blood counts are abnormally low.

combination chemotherapy: A combination of two or more chemical agents to optimize cancer cell death. Often referred to as "chemo cocktails."

combined modality therapy: Two or more types of therapies used in conjunction, or alternating, with the purpose of optimizing cancer cell death.

complete blood count (CBC, also known as **myelogram):** A series of lab tests that usually include a count of red blood cells, white blood cells, platelets, hemoglobin, and other components of blood.

Cooper's ligaments (suspensory ligaments of the breast, or **of Cooper):** Fibrous, flexible strands of tissue that attach the breast glands to the muscles of the chest wall (pectoralis muscles) and that shape and support the breasts.

core biopsy: A biopsy procedure in which a large needle is inserted in the breast to obtain a piece of a suspicious lump for diagnosis. See also **biopsy**.

cyst: An abnormal sac containing gas, liquid, or semisolid material, bounded by a membranous lining. Some lumps that are found in the breast turn out to be cysts, especially in premenopausal women, and are usually benign.

cytotoxic: Something that prevents or inhibits normal cell function, or is destructive to cells. In reference to cancer, it usually describes agents used in chemo.

CTZ (chemotactic trigger zone): A small region in the brain that triggers nausea and vomiting. Many chemo agents are known to stimulate this area.

D

diagnosis: The identification by a physician of a condition or disease based on the signs and symptoms that a patient presents.

differentiation: The characteristics of a cell that mark its development. In a cancer cell, the degree of differentiation can potentially predict the degree of its aggressiveness.

DNA (deoxyribonucleic acid): A substance found mainly in the nuclei of human, animal, and plant cells. Its purpose is to automatically reproduce chromosomes and viruses, and it contains all the genetic information needed to reproduce another functioning cell.

ductal carcinoma in situ (DCIS) (also known as **intraductal** or **non-invasive breast cancer):** A cancer of the breast that is confined to its original site in the lining of the duct of the breast gland.

dysphagia: Difficulty in swallowing.

E

edema: The retention of excess fluid in the body, a body part, or organ. See **lymphedema.**

endocrine manipulation: A treatment whereby an individual's hormonal balance is altered. In breast cancer, this type of treatment may be employed if the cancer is hormone-dependent.

erythrocytes: Red blood cells whose job is to deliver oxygen to the body's tissues.

estrogen: A female sex hormone secreted by the ovaries. Among its functions are promoting menstruation, reproduction, and stimulating secondary sex characteristics in developing women. For patients whose breast cancer is hormone receptive, the level of estrogen may be manipulated by drugs.

estrogen receptor (ER): A protein (receptor molecule) to which estrogen will attach.

estrogen receptor assay (ERA): A test done on cancerous tissue, along with a **progesterone receptor assay**, to see if a breast cancer is hormone-dependent and thus may be treated with hormonal therapy.

excisional biopsy: See **biopsy.**

external (-beam) radiation: A type of radiation which delivers a beam of high-energy rays (usually X rays) to the cancer site.

F

familial cancer: A cancer that is thought to have occurred for genetic reasons, ie., it is inherited.

fat necrosis tumor: A hard, noncancerous lump that may develop due to trauma or injury to the breast and which may have caused fat-cell death.

fibroadenoma: A benign (noncancerous) neoplasm composed of spindle- or star-shaped cells and connective tissue. This condition commonly occurs in breast tissue and is most often found in younger women.

fibrocystic breast changes or **condition** or **disease:** A nonmalignant condition in which there are cystic lesions that develop within a noticeable amount of fibrous connective tissue in the breast. This may cause the breast to feel lumpy, and discomfort may be heightened by the menstrual cycle.

fine needle aspiration: A procedure in which a small needle is used to remove cells or fluid from tissue. See also **aspiration**.

flow cytometry: A test that counts and categorizes cells. In relation to cancer, it may be done to determine how "aggressive" a malignant cancer is.

frozen section: A tissue sample that has been frozen rapidly, thinly cut, and stained for examination under a microscope by a pathologist. See also **permanent section**.

G

gene: The basic unit of heredity, located in a specific position on a chromosome in the nucleus of the cell. Under normal circumstances, it can reproduce itself precisely and is able to control the function of other genetic material such as proteins so that vital information may be transmitted from one cell to another.

generic name: The nonmarketed name for a drug. Most drugs have both a generic and one or more brand names, although consumers are more familiar with the latter.

H

hematoma: A collection of blood that is generally confined to one area, within an organ, tissue, or spaces within the body. This can result from injury, trauma, or at a wound site.

HER-2/neu (human epidermal growth factor receptor 2): An oncoprotein that resides on the cell surface and stimulates its growth. Small amounts are found on the surface of normal breast cells, but in some cases of breast cancer (approximately 25 to 30 percent) there is an excess of the protein, which can cause the cancer to be more aggressive. In addition, this name refers to the gene for the cell surface protein. The gene can be amplified, meaning the cell has excess copies of it in its nucleus or center.

hormonal therapy: A type of cancer treatment that uses hormones to control the growth of cancer. Hormonal therapies may include estrogens, progestins, and androgens. See also **tamoxifen**.

hormone receptor assay: Diagnostic tests to determine if a patient is a candidate for hormonal therapy. It is performed on tumor samples removed during biopsy.

hormones: Chemical substances that are produced and secreted by various organs to help regulate growth, metabolism, and reproduction. Common female hormones: estrogen, progesterone, prolactin. Steroid hormones include androgens (male sex hormones) and estrogens (female sex hormones). Some hormones are used as treatment following surgery for cancer.

hot flashes: Usually a symptom of menopause that also presents itself sometimes in patients undergoing chemo for breast cancer. It is characterized by perspiration and sudden feelings of heat and flushing.

hyperplasia (atypical): A benign (noncancerous) growth of cells of breast tissue that slightly increases the risk of breast cancer.

I

immune system: The complex body system that is the main defense against infection and disease.

immunology: The branch of science that is concerned with the study of sensitivity to substances and allergies.

immunosuppressed: A condition in which the ability of the immune system to fight off disease and infection has been interfered with so that natural responses cannot occur, thereby increasing the chances of infection. This condition is often induced by chemo because of the drug's destructive effects on the body's cells, especially white blood cells.

immunotherapy (also known as **biological therapy, biological response modifier [BRM] therapy**): Any treatment that alters the body's reaction to disease such that it fortifies or restores the defense mechanisms of the immune system.

infiltrating cancer (also known as **invading, invasive cancer**): A malignancy that has spread past its origin into surrounding tissue.

inflammation: A reaction of tissue to various causes that may exhibit pain, redness, or warmth. It may be a side effect of radiation therapy.

inflammatory response: When tissue is damaged, the redness, warmth, swelling, and pain at the site of injury by radiation. See also **ulcerization**.

informed consent: Voluntary (usually written) consent given by a patient before agreeing to a medical procedure or participating in a clinical trial.

in situ: A term denoting "in place," meaning that the cancer is still confined to its area of origin. If the cancer is in situ, it is in its early stages.

internal radiation (implant radiation, brachytherapy): A type of radiation therapy that is administered into or near the tumor itself. The radioactive material is usually sealed in needles, seeds, wires, or catheters.

intramuscular (IM): A method of administering medication by needle into a muscle.

intravenous (IV): A method of administering medication by a needle into a vein.

invasive cancer: See **infiltrating cancer.**

invasive (infiltrating) ductal carcinoma: A cancer that begins in the lining of the ducts of the mammary glands and spreads to areas outside the gland. This is the most common form of breast cancer.

invasive procedure: Any procedure or surgery that entails inserting an instrument through the skin or a body opening for purposes of diagnosis or treatment.

inverted nipple: The turning inward of a nipple. It is a possible sign of breast cancer but is usually congenital, meaning that it occurred naturally without an underlying pathologic process.

J–L

lactation: The production of breast milk, or the period following childbirth when the mother produces breast milk.

lesion: A wound or injury site. In cancer patients, a lesion can also mean the area of tissue that is affected by disease.

leukocytes: Also known as white blood cells or corpuscles. They are the blood cells that help fight infection, and are the main line of defense in the body's immune system. Leukocytes are the only blood cells that cannot be replenished by transfusion.

leukopenia (also known as **leukocytopenia**): The condition in which there is an abnormally low number of white blood cells (leukocytes), often following chemo. The result of this condition is increased susceptibility to infection.

liver scan (also known as **scintiscan**): The image of the liver produced on film or on a computer screen with the aid of injected radioactive substances.

lobes: The fifteen to twenty subdivisions of the mammary gland (breast) that are connected (radiating centrally) but distinct. They comprise the body of the gland, and are located within the breast tissue. Each lobe drains into a single duct.

lobular: Pertaining to the part of the breast that is farthest from the nipple. See **lobules**.

lobules: Subdivisions of the lobes of the mammary gland.

localized cancer: A cancer that has not yet spread, and is at the site of origin. See also **in situ**.

lump: Any abnormal mass of tissue in the body that may or may not be malignant.

lumpectomy: See **segmental mastectomy** under **mastectomy** heading.

lymph: The clear fluid containing white blood cells and antibodies that circulates throughout the body in the **lymphatic system**.

lymphangitis: Infection of the lymph channels.

lymphatic system: A network of thin-walled vessels that runs throughout the body. These vessels drain fluid (lymph), which carries waste products and bacteria from between cells, emptying into the vascular (blood) system. The lymph nodes are also part of this system.

lymphedema: A chronic condition in which there is excess swelling in the extremities because of fluid retention. In breast-cancer patients, secondary lymphedema in the arm may be a result of infection, the blockage of vessels by malignancies, or the lack of sufficient vessels following surgery.

lymph nodes (also known as **lymph glands**): Rounded tissues of the lymphatic system that produce lymphocytes and monocytes (white blood cells) and filter out bacteria and cancer cells from the bloodstream. They can also be the site of metastatic disease.

lymphocytes: A kind of leukocyte (white blood cell).

M

macrocyst: A cyst that is large enough to be palpable or visible to the naked eye.

magnetic resonance imaging (MRI, also known as **nuclear magnetic resonance imaging, NMR imaging, nuclear magnetic resonance tomography):** A noninvasive diagnostic tool employing nuclear resonance technology to offer a picture of internal tissue.

malignant tumor: A neoplasm that is composed of cancerous cells. These cells are characterized by uncontrolled growth and invasion of surrounding cells, and have the ability to metastasize, spreading to areas remote from the primary growth.

mammary glands: The breasts that develop on the chests of adult females. The glands contain lobules that secrete milk, which empty into ducts to the nipple.

mammogram: The image on X-ray film generated by a mammography. It is commonly used as a means of screening for (but not diagnosing) early breast cancer, and can detect microcalcifications up to two years before they would otherwise be palpable. It is recommended that most women obtain a baseline mammogram at the age of forty as a means of comparison for later mammograms.

margins: The border of tissue surrounding a tumor.

mastalgia (also known as **mastodynia, mammalgia**): Pain along the nerves supplied to the breast (mammary neuralgia). The pain can feel like severe throbbing or stabbing.

mastectomy (also known as **mammmectomy**): The surgical removal of the breast. These are the types:

- **extended radical mastectomy:** Removal of the entire breast plus chest (pectoral) muscles and some lymphatic tissue.
- **modified radical mastectomy:** Removal of the entire breast and some lymph nodes. The pectoral muscles are preserved. This is the most common type of mastectomy.
- **prophylactic (preventative) mastectomy:** Removal of breast tissue in patients before the onset of cancer. It is a preventative measure chosen by some patients who have a marked (genetic) predisposition for getting cancer.
- **radical mastectomy** (also known as **Halsted operation, radical**): Removal of the entire breast plus pectoral muscles, some lymph nodes, and other surrounding tissues.

- **segmental mastectomy (partial mastectomy/ lumpectomy):** Surgical removal of either a benign or malignant lesion plus surrounding tissue, with conservation of as much of the breast as possible.
- **simple (total) mastectomy:** Removal of the breast including the nipple, areola, and some of the overlying skin.
- **skin-sparing mastectomy:** A fairly new procedure that preserves as much breast tissue as possible. It is a combined procedure in which the surgeon's work is followed by reconstruction by a plastic surgeon.

mastitis: An inflammation of the breast due to infection that can be treated with antibiotics.

menopause: The time in a woman's life when the menstrual cycle has permanently ceased, usually beginning between the ages of forty-five to fifty-five. During menopause, the ovaries produce lower levels of the hormone estrogen. The hormonal imbalances may produce symptoms such as hot flashes, sweating, and headaches. Temporary or permanent menopause can also be induced by chemotherapy (chemopause).

metastasis: The spread of disease from one part of the body to another. In cancer, this means that growth of new neoplasms has occurred remote from the original tumor site (primary tumor). Metastasis of cancers may have resulted from the spread of broken-off tumor cells via the lymphatic system or the bloodstream. The metastasis is of the same type as the original cancer; for example, if breast cancer has metastasized to the liver, it is still referred to as breast cancer. The plural form is metastases.

microcalcifications: Pieces of hardened tissue that appear on mammograms as small spots. They require follow-up to determine whether they are benign or malignant.

microcyst: A tiny cyst in the breast that is too small to be seen or palpated, but which may be detected on a mammogram or by ultrasound.

micrometastasis: The stage of metastasis where the secondary tumors cannot be detected by routine clinical screening.

myelosuppressed: The state in which there is a decrease in the ability of the bone marrow to produce blood cells. This condition may heighten vulnerability to infection and disease, and may produce fatigue.

N

needle biopsy: Procedure in which a tissue sample is removed from the breast with a needle and suction. The sample is then examined to determine if the cells are cancerous. See also **aspiration.**

neoplasm (also known as **tumor, growth**): Abnormal growth of tissue that is caused by faster than normal proliferation of cells. Neoplasms grow uncontrolled and in an uncoordinated fashion, and most likely will form a mass known as a tumor. The tumor may be benign (non-cancerous) or malignant (cancerous). However, the term most often refers to a cancerous growth.

neutrophils: Particles that make up 60 percent of all white blood cells. Their job is to interrupt and destroy bacteria. They are a type of leukocyte.

nodule (also known as **nodulus**): A small mass of solid tissue.

O

occult disease: Cancer that is present but in amounts too small to be detected.

oncogene: A gene that normally directs proteins involved in cell growth or regulation but may, if mutated, trigger or aid the proliferation of cancerous cells. See also **BRCA-1.**

oncologist: A physician whose specialty is cancer treatment. See also **oncology.**

oncology: The branch of medical science dealing with the biological, physical, and chemical properties and aspects of neoplasms. It also includes the study of the causes and course of disease, and treatments involved.

one-step procedure: A procedure in which a surgical biopsy is performed under general anesthesia. If the biopsy concludes that cancer is present, then a mastectomy or lumpectomy is performed immediately following the biopsy as part of one surgical operation.

oophorectomy (also known as **ovariectomy**)**:** A surgical procedure to remove the ovaries. It may be employed as a part of hormone therapy to limit the body's production of estrogen.

osteoporosis: Condition in which there is a reduction in the quantity of bone or an atrophy of skeletal tissue that is usually age-related. It is characterized by decreased bone mass and increased vulnerability to bone fractures. Postmenopausal women are at highest risk.

P

palliative treatment: Therapy whose purpose is to reduce or relieve symptoms of a disease, but which does not affect or cure the underlying disease itself. Such therapy should help pain and other symptoms.

palpation: The use of hands to examine organs, masses, or to detect abnormalities. Your physician will palpate the breast to check for lumps (palpable masses).

pathology: The specialty of medicine that deals with all aspects of disease. Pathological examination must be carried out to determine whether a tumor is cancerous.

pathologist: A physician trained to make diagnoses from tissue samples.

pectoralis (pectoral) muscles: Muscular tissue attached to the front of the chest wall and extending to the upper arms. Commonly referred to as the chest muscles.

permanent section: A diagnostic technique in which a thinly sliced biopsy sample is put on a slide for examination by microscope.

planning session: See **simulation session.**

platelets (thrombocytes): Disk-shaped structures in the blood fluid that are necessary for clotting. They are formed in the bone marrow by fragmentation of larger cells, and travel in the bloodstream.

polychemotherapy: Another term for combination chemo or "chemo cocktails."

precancer (also known as **premalignant**)**:** A lesion from which there is the likelihood of developing a malignant neoplasm.

progesterone: A female hormone that is an anti-estrogenic steroid produced naturally by the female body and also synthetically used to correct menstrual periods and in contraception.

progesterone receptor assay (PRA): A test that determines if breast cancer cells have the progesterone receptor and are therefore hormone dependent for growth.

prognosis: An educated prediction made by a physician as to the course or outcome of a disease.

prolactin (PRL): A female protein hormone which stimulates the secretion of milk and possibly breast growth during pregnancy.

prophylactic mastectomy: See **mastectomy.**

prosthesis: An artificial body form. For mastectomy patients, a breast prosthesis may be worn inside the bra to make the surgery undetectable. Chemo patients who purchase a wig may be covered by medical insurance if a doctor writes them a prescription for a hair prosthesis.

protocol: The detailed schedule and components of a patient's course of treatment.

pus: A collection of dead neutrophils, monocytes, bacteria, and tissue.

Q–R

radiation oncologist: A physician whose specialty is the use of radiation to treat cancer.

radiation pneumonitis: Inflammation of the lungs caused by radiation to the chest.

radiation recall: An inflammatory reaction to radiation therapy characterized by redness, swelling, and peeling at the treatment site, and in rare cases, blistering occurring after (sometimes long after) the treatment is completed and usually instigated by the use of certain chemotherapy agents.

radiation therapy: See **radiotherapy**.

radioactivity: The emission of radiation which can include alpha particles, nucleons, electrons, and gamma rays.

radiologist: A physician who specializes in diagnoses of diseases by the use of X rays, radionuclides, nuclear magnetic resonance imaging (NMR). A diagnostic radiologist may also be trained in the use of magnetic resonance imaging (MRI) and diagnostic unltrasound.

radionuclide: A substance (atomic) that is produced naturally or artificially and which is characterized by its radioactivity.

radiotherapy: A type of cancer treatment that employs the use of high-energy radiation to destroy cancer cells. Radiation therapy may be used to shrink the size of a tumor before surgery or to destroy any lingering cancer cells after surgery.

reconstructive surgery: A surgical procedure that involves fashioning a breast out of available tissue from the patient, or with use of a breast implant.

recurrence: A reappearance of cancer following a period of remission.

red blood cells: See **erythrocytes**.

regional cancer (also known as **regional involve-**

ment): The spread of cancer beyond its original site to surrounding areas, but still contained in one general location. If breast cancer has spread to the lymph nodes or chest wall, there is regional cancer.

rehabilitation: Programs that help patients adjust and return to full, productive lives. May involve physical therapy, the use of a prosthesis, counseling, and emotional support.

remission: The period during which there is partial improvement or complete disappearance of the cancer.

retraction: The process of skin pulling back, or shrinking of, breast tissue that can look like dimpling. This is a warning sign to see a doctor.

risk factors: Things that may predispose an individual to a disease, or which increase the chance of being afflicted. In breast cancer, risk factors include familial breast disease, a high-fat diet, early onset of menses, late menopause, no biological children, or having a first child after the age of thirty. Note that risk factors do not determine whether an individual will get a certain disease.

S

secondary tumor: A tumor that develops as a consequence of metastasis, away from the original or primary cancer site.

simulation session: After the initial consultation with a radiology oncologist, this is the planning session in which preparatory procedures are made for radiation therapy, such as making a body mold and marking the area to be treated.

staging: The process of determining the extent of the cancer based on certain characteristics, including whether the cancer has metastasized. In breast cancer, it is determined by whether the lymph nodes are involved, whether the cancer has spread to other parts of the body, and the size of the tumor. Five different stages (stage 0–stage IV) are used in breast cancer with sublevels in each stage, with stage IV the most serious.

stellate: Star-like shapes on some mammograms that may or may not be associated with malignant conditions.

stereotactic needle biopsy (also known as **mammotest):** A biopsy performed on the breast while it is compressed in a mammographic procedure. Information is gathered from the images produced to direct a needle to the lump's position to obtain a biopsy sample.

stomatitis: Inflammation of the mouth which may produce discomfort and may be prone to infection (mouth sores). A common side effect of chemo.

T

tamoxifen: A synthetic, nonsteroidal antiestrogen drug that is used in prevention and treatment of breast-cancer patients. Women taking tamoxifen are at increased risk of endometrial carcinoma, deep venous thrombosis, pulmonary embolism, and cataracts. The danger is greatest in women over the age of fifty. Tamoxifen is usually taken for up to five years.

thrombocytopenia: Abnormally low numbers of platelets in the blood as a result of bone marrow suppression. This may result in the increased risk of hemorrhages and the inablity of blood to clot. This condition is a possible side effect of chemo or radiation therapy.

tissue: A collection of similar cells and the cellular material surrounding them. The four basic tissues in the human body are: epithelium, connective tissues (blood, bone, cartilage), muscle tissue, and nerve tissue. Much of the breast is composed of adipose (fat) tissue.

tissue expander: A device used in reconstructive surgery of the breast. It is an inflatable, balloonlike implant filled with saline, in which the volume can be varied after implantation through a port that protrudes from the breast. The purpose is to slowly stretch the muscle and/or skin of the breast area so it can later be replaced with a permanent implant filled with saline or silicone.

tram flap: Abbreviation term for the transverse rectus abdominus musculocutaneous flap. This is a term used in reconstructive surgery. It is a method that uses tissue from the patient's lower abdomen to reshape the surgically removed breast. In this procedure, the tissue from the lower abdomen is still attached to the central abdominal muscles so that blood flow to the transferred tissue is maintained.

tumor: See **neoplasm.**

two-step procedure: Two separate surgeries for purposes of surgical biopsy and breast surgery.

U–Z

ulcerization: Shallow sores created as a result of sloughing off dead tissue at the radiation site.

ultrasound examination (diagnostic ultrasound): The use of high-frequency sound waves (frequency greater than 30,000 Hz) to generate two-dimensional diagnostic images. The examination will help determine whether the tumor is solid or fluid-filled by the measurement of reflection or absorption of the sound waves.

ultrasound-guided biopsy: The employment of ultrasound to guide a physician in obtaining a tissue sample with a biopsy needle.

vascular access device: A device implanted with a port so that blood samples and chemo administration may be expedited. These devices eliminate the need for repeated needle injection during chemo.

ABOUT THE AUTHOR

JAMI BERNARD is an award-winning film critic for the *New York Daily News* and author of four film books: *First Films*, *Total Exposure*, *Quentin Tarantino: The Man and His Movies*, and *Chick Flicks*. She is a member and former chair of the New York Film Critics Circle, and a member of the National Society of Film Critics. In addition to radio, TV, and Internet-radio appearances, she writes the Cancer Girl column for *Mamm* magazine.

Visit the author at http://www.jamibernard.com